Barry Coughlan was born in Cork in 1953. While at school in Presentation Brothers' College, Cork, he developed a keen interest in rugby, which, he claims, is the greatest team game in the world. For the past twelve years he has been a journalist with the *Cork Examiner* group, involved in both news and sports reporting. Three years ago, he was appointed chief rugby correspondent. He has covered international rugby at senior, "B" and schools levels, travelling many times to the home countries, France and Romania on these assignments. A long-time admirer of the All Blacks, whom he has reported on during their tours to the Northern Hemisphere, he travelled to New Zealand to cover the 1983 British and Irish Lions tour.

Cover photo shows David Irwin making one of the Lions' rare breaks in the fourth test at Auckland (Des Barry).

THE IRISH LIONS
1896~1983

BARRY COUGHLAN

WARD
RIVER
PRESS

A Paperback Original
First published 1983 by
Ward River Press Ltd.,
Knocksedan House,
Swords, Co. Dublin, Ireland

ISBN 0 907085 67 9

Cover design by Steven Hope
Typeset by Inset Ltd.,
171 Drimnagh Road, Dublin 12.
Printed by Mount Salus Limited,
Tritonville Road, Dublin 4.

To Margaret, Lynda and Sarah,
for their patience and understanding

ACKNOWLEDGEMENTS

This book, the story of the Irish Lions since 1896, might never have been undertaken by me were it not for the encouragement and advice of some of my close working colleagues. I need not mention names, for they know who they are.

I would like to pay particular thanks to the directors of my company, *The Cork Examiner,* for sending me to New Zealand to cover the 1983 Lions tour, for the end product could never have materialised without first-hand coverage of that. And for their help in many other ways, I owe them further gratitude.

To those former and present Irish Lions who afforded me their time and gave me the information I sought on previous tours, I would also proffer sincere thanks.

Many of the modern-day photographs used in the book have been taken by Des Barry, a *Cork Examiner* colleague, who covered part of the tour to New Zealand. Others have come from the *Cork Examiner* files, while more were supplied by New Zealand and South African newspapers and I would like to thank in particular the *Dominion,* the *New Zealand Times* and the *Wellington Post,* all part of the Wellington Newspapers Group, the *New Zealand Herald, Auckland, Rugby News* (New Zealand), the *Cape Times* and also the former players who supplied photographs from their personal files.

Barry Coughlan
August 1983

CONTENTS

Page

LIST OF ILLUSTRATIONS

Harry McKibbin at Kroonstaad Bowling Green, 1938
The Irish Contingent in South Africa, 1938
Jackie Kyle and Tom Clifford in New Zealand, 1950
Tom Clifford and Karl Mullen at Otago
Tony O'Reilly and Bill Mulcahy, 1959
Lord Wakefield with Noel Murphy and Andy Mulligan
Mike Gibson in New Zealand, 1966
Noel Murphy, Willie John McBride, Ronnie Lamont and
    Ray McLoughlin
Roger Young with Mick Doyle and Jeff Young in South
    Africa, 1968
Willie John McBride in Natal, 1968
The Irish team against Scotland, 1960
Don Clarke and Bob Scott of New Zealand
Noel Murphy, John O'Driscoll and Phil Orr in South Africa
Willie Duggan in 1977
David Irwin at the Triple Crown match against Wales, 1982
Tom Kiernan and Michael Kiernan
John O'Driscoll with Welshman Terry Holmes, 1982
Gareth Davies and Trevor Ringland at Lansdowne Road
Trevor Ringland, David Irwin and Gareth Davies
Moss Keane and Maurice Colclough
Gary Pearce with Ciaran Fitzgerald and Willie Duggan
Triple Crown winners at Lansdowne Road, 1982
Ollie Campbell in the first test at Christchurch, June 1983
The test front row: Graham Price, Ciaran Fitzgerald and
    Staff Jones
Donal Lenihan in action against Hawkes Bay
Lions tourists in New Zealand, 1983
Michael Kiernan with Allan Hewson of Wellington
All Black Dave Loveridge and Ciaran Fitzgerald
David Irwin in Southland, June 1983
Ollie Campbell and John Rutherford in Dunedin

FOREWORD
by Tony O'Reilly

The nature of rugby football is that it is a game for gentlemen of all classes to be played for enjoyment. Lions tours have enabled players to perfect and polish and associate in a way which one does not always get at other times in life.

The Lions should represent the highest form of the art, which is about running the ball. It is not essentially about winning, rather about the beauty of rugby football, about moving the ball from both forwards and backs. When people lose sight of this, and subjugate the notion of the greatness, the purity and the visual attraction of rugby to the notion of winning, then you end up in a miasma of statistics.

I believe Lions teams should never be determined to win at all costs, but they should be determined to parade all the great skills of the game. And if I have one criticism of the coaching system of the game today, it is that some of the spontaneity that made Lions teams memorable through the last fifty years and more is missing.

The tragedy of the 1983 tour was that they had no Ken Jones, no Jack Kyle or Bleddyn Williams, no Cliff Morgan, Jeff Butterfield, W.P.C. Davies, no Malcolm Price, Dave Hewitt, Bev Risman, Peter Jackson, David Duckham, Gerald Davies, John Dawes or Barry John. Recent times have seen a progression towards anonymity.

The essential attraction of rugby is running. I would prefer to go out on a tour with a commitment to that philosophy and lose the game, rather than engage in a featureless trench warfare of packs battling and winning by the preponderance of the place kick. What price have we paid for the dedication to winning, what price have we paid for our reliance on ten-man rugby? The Lions should always exemplify the best of running rugby; and if they lose that, then they have lost their commitment to excellence.

I do not rank the recent tour to New Zealand as utter failure, as some might see it. The greatness, which has eluded some commentators, was the way in which the team, under extraordinary pressure and criticism, maintained their dignity. This was exemplified in particular by Ciaran Fitzgerald. What certain people expected of him is beyond me, because some things are outside a captain's control. He cannot cause the wings to run any faster; he cannot give a man a side-step if the man does not have one. I was surprised and disappointed at the way the function of the captaincy on the field was exaggerated by certain sections of the British press in order to impugn the man.

A Lions captain should not be the actual tactician of the tour. He will of course be a competent player, but his biggest contribution is the dignity and capacity with which he comports himself off the field. In the light of that criterion, I believe Fitzgerald had a fine tour.

No Lions tour is complete without the Irish. The extraordinary fact is that since Lions sides have been going abroad in contemporary times, we have produced eight captains.

It is clear that there is something unique about Ireland and about the Irish personality which lends itself easily to the notion of leadership to a group of people from the four home countries.

The probability is that in its truest sense, rugby is a more democratic game in Ireland than anywhere else. It tends to be a class game in England and to a degree in Scotland, although again the Borders and the High School boys of the Rift Valley represent different classes. Because of that, the people who play rugby for Ireland tend to be more cosmopolitan, more rounded and perhaps less restricted in their attitudes than those from England, Scotland or Wales. There is, I believe, a certain provincialism bred out of the competitiveness of the United Kingdom, fostering antagonisms of which the Irish are happily free. Therefore Irish players move more easily in the international group, and Irish captains captain more easily. That is not to say that English, Scots or Welsh are not acceptable!

Irish rugby tends to produce more characters — more Tom Cliffords, more Tom Reids, to whom people can respond amiably. The Irish are a friendly, charming people and I think that the combination of ordinariness and sophistication has produced a prototype of the Irishman on tour which is very enriching. It can be of the highly literate and witty level of a Mulligan or a Pedlow, at the more homely level of a Clifford or Reid, or at the executive level of a Mullen, Dawson or Kiernan, but we seem to combine all the elements that go to make a touring side. We like to think that the Irish are good all rounders. Inherently we are a charming people, although we can also be very treacherous — and I'm not sure if that goes hand in hand with charm! We seem to know what people would like to hear, and how to articulate it persuasively. That is a useful skill in its own way.

I would like to think that no Lions tour could go away without a strong Irish contingent, and that the best of the Lions teams would have a large Irish contingent — assuming of course that the players themselves match their off-the-field talents. That is something which has to be spoken to in the particular, not in the generality, although the past has shown it, in fact, to be a generality.

Tony O'Reilly
August 1983

CHAPTER 1

THE HISTORY OF THE LIONS

For rugby fans in Australia, New Zealand and South Africa, there is nothing quite like the Lions, the team comprised of Irish, English, Welsh and Scotsmen who come together every few years to undertake a major overseas tour. Strange, isn't it, when one considers the Lions' record? Australia has always been a happy hunting ground but in the more dodgy territories of New Zealand and South Africa, success has been hard to come by. In 1971 the Lions broke new ground in New Zealand when Welshman John Dawes captained them to their first series win there, and three years later, Willie John McBride captained a side to victory in South Africa. Touring sides from Britain and Ireland had tasted success in South Africa long before that, but from 1910 onwards, when the trips became official expeditions, they had received no joy whatever.

Yet wherever they go, win or lose, the Lions attract attention from the media and from the public. They are, in many respects, the team everyone wants to play.

New Zealand journalist T. P. McLean wrote recently: "It's curious that great matches played by the Lions on their five tours to this country since 1950 are easier to remember than memorable achievements by All Blacks and other teams against them. It may be that the speed, skill and audacity of most of the Lions teams have made them easier to recall than the orthodox play so often based upon superlative forward strength of many New Zealand teams."

Times have changed somewhat, in New Zealand at least,

where after the 1971 series defeat, the All Blacks changed their policy and are now committed to a 15-man game, while in the past few years in Britain and Ireland, back play, at least compared with the old days, has deteriorated.

Yet the Lions still have a magnetic attraction for the people of New Zealand and, for rugby and other reasons, for the South Africans. Like the All Blacks, the Springboks and to a lesser degree, the Wallabies, they are a major money-spinner for the host countries and for its various unions.

Of all touring sides, the Lions are distinctly unique because they never play at home. Some people are of the opinion that this is wrong. The punters in Britain and Ireland follow their movements on foreign soil with avid interest, and newspaper, radio, and television coverage in the last decade has never been greater. Yet only the lucky ones, those who can afford to join the ever-increasing numbers of supporters' groups, see them in the flesh. It has been claimed that the Lions would lose their appeal if they were to play here; those holding that view point out that when touring sides travel to the Northern hemisphere there is more than enough competition by way of the Irish, English, Scottish and Welsh national sides, and from the Barbarians, the home version of the Lions. The question of whether they should or should not play at home has been a matter of debate among rugby fans for some time and no doubt will continue to be so, although I doubt if the situation will ever change.

Another debate which has been prevalent concerns the future of the Lions. As a result of increasing pressures on International players, there has been a change in thinking since 1980, when the tour itinerary was reduced to 18 matches. That followed the 1977 tour to New Zealand and Fiji when the Lions played 26 games on a trip which was ruined by appalling weather. The most recent trip to New Zealand was not spoiled by the same climatic conditions, but the duration of the tour did pose problems for the tourists. It is obvious that when men from four different nations get together for the first time various difficulties arise. The Lions had hardly had time to find a blend when they were faced with the first test. Yet at the same time, longer tours, as experienced in 1977, are really no longer acceptable for a variety of reasons. In an amateur game, where players have to adopt a professional approach to survive, the pressures on time can sometimes be unbearable. The majority of players are employees, not employers, and therefore have to request time off work with pay. There are many kind employers who willingly allow their men several weeks' paid leave in order to pursue their rugby careers. It is, in some respects, an honour for those companies too; and having top class rugby players on their pay rolls can bring them valuable business.

Lions' players, like their predecessors, receive an allowance each day for out-of-pocket expenses. The present rate is £8 sterling, which is fairly sufficient for their needs, as accommodation and food is supplied on the tour. One prominent player with whom I spoke was critical of the four home unions, saying that they should be in a position to approach employers and offer to pay players' wages:

> Some players over the years have had to give up their jobs for the honour of becoming Lions. It is an honour to be asked and for everyone, particularly first-timers, the realisation of a lifetime's dream. It does not seem fair that some have to give up jobs and then take the risk that they will get another at home. The players are the money-spinners. I am not advocating professional rugby but I believe the pressure should be taken away from them. In addition, would not the four home unions then be able to send out a much stronger team on tour? One has only to look back on previous tours to realise how many players were unavailable because they could not approach their employers seeking paid leave.

These are problems which have been compounded in recent

years, but there are still enough men in the four home countries willing to tour at any cost and if some think that Lions tours will eventually be phased out, I believe we will see such touring sides for many years to come at any rate.

The honour of becoming a Lion knows no bounds and the experience gained on an overseas tour is generally appreciated by the players. Shortly after being dropped for the third test on this year's tour, Irishman Hugo MacNeill, reflecting on the tour up to that point, told me, "You cannot compare a few bad results with the experience one gains on a trip of this nature."

The selection process is a long one which begins many months before the start of the tour. Some of the key players will have been earmarked for a long time before selection, but the real work starts with the appointment of the selectors, five in number, including the tour manager and coach, who would have already been issued with their portfolios.

For the 1983 tour, the additional selectors, Brian O'Brien, (Ireland), Rhys Williams (Wales) and John Finlan (England), were named on August 1982, and from then until the party was finalised, they put in hundreds of hours, travelling all over Britain and Ireland and attending selection committee meetings.

They met first in early September 1982 where the ground rules, as it were, were laid down. They spoke about the concept of the tour, about the quality of the opposition and about the type of player that would be required. Each man selected would be expected to operate efficiently in his own position and to be a good traveller. Players noted for homesickness were not discounted, but if there were a 50-50 chance between two players, then the man who travelled best, would normally get the vote.

The selection of the 1983 Lions was beset with difficulties, concedes selector O'Brien, because the home international series had been so closely contested and because there was so little to choose between a number of players.

In the months after his appointment, O'Brien was on

the move almost every weekend. When not "spying" for the Lions, he was away on duties as a Munster and Irish selector and he reviewed the vast majority of some 160 players who were being considered. Realistically, the number of players in with a fighting chance was much, much, less than that, but each player had to'be seen all the same.

Several meetings later, the selectors had the "bones" of a side, but it was the international championship which settled most of the positions, and the question of who was to go and who was not to go. The party was not actually finalised until the final whistle had gone in the last match. For O'Brien and two of his colleagues, the work had been done, seven months of it, and perhaps his only disappointment was that he would not be there to see them play. Lions selectors, apart from management, are not invited on tour.

An interesting feature of the history of the Lions is that it was not until 1924 that they were so called. New Zealand and South Africa had been nicknamed prior to that. When a British and Irish side went to South Africa in 1924, the symbol they used, which portrayed a lion, was the same as that of a British military regiment. The South African newspapers, anxious to add colour to the occasion picked it up and from then on they have had the Lions tag.

Nowadays the Lions are clad in scarlet jerseys, white shorts, and navy stockings with a green turnover, representing the colours of the four home unions, but the first touring sides wore red, white and blue striped jerseys, white shorts and red stockings. The colours were later changed to blue jerseys, white shorts and red stockings but before the 1930 tour to New Zealand, the Irish protested and a green elasticated flash was added to the hose. That outfit brought a howl of protest from the New Zealand players, who had to play in white gear in the test games, thus appearing as "All Whites". And so, after the setting up of the four home unions tours committee in 1949 the Lions travelled to New Zealand a year later, this time outfitted in the regalia which remains their identification today.

CHAPTER 2

RUGBY IN IRELAND

Believe it or not, over 100 countries throughout the world play Rugby Union in an organised fashion, some merely on a club basis but the majority on a National scale as well.

When talking about rugby, most people tend to think first of the four home countries, England, Scotland, Ireland and Wales, then of France, New Zealand, South Africa, Australia, Argentina and Romania with perhaps Canada and the US also springing to mind.

But what about Andorra, one of the world's smallest nations with one club and 150 players? What about Bahrain with a similar number, Liberia and Malawi with 200 each, Nigeria with 400, Israel with 450, Bulgaria with 1,000, India with 1,250, Thailand, South Korea and Belgium with 1,500, Chile with 2,500, Holland with 4,800 or Portugal with 5,700?

We may never see or hear of the progress of the game in those countries, but rest assured that in most the game is growing. It might come as a surprise that there are more people playing rugby in such countries as Japan, Italy, Russia, Spain and Fiji than there are in Ireland but it is a fact. In some cases the difference in numbers is astounding.

One can understand how Japan, with its population of 115 million, should have huge numbers playing rugby, even if it is a minority sport, but a staggering comparison is that between the 1971 figures (60,000) and the figures a decade later (180,000). Fiji may have only a total population of just over half a million, yet there are more involved in the game (11,000) than in Ireland. Russia has 45,000 players, Italy 15,000 and Spain 11,800, while the playing strength of Canada for instance is 10,000.

Compare the playing population within Ireland (10,000) to that in England (300,000), South Africa (215,000), France and New Zealand (170,000 each), Wales (40,000) and Scotland (25,000). Our record in International terms is not bad at all!

Ireland's playing record against Scotland and France is 48.3 and 48.2 per cent respectively while the percentages against England (40) and Wales (35.8) drag our average in the championship down to 42.70 per cent, still healthy enough. Include matches against New Zealand, South Africa and Australia and the average slips slightly again to 41.62 per cent, although the individual record against Australia, a similarly sized Rugby Union playing nation is 66.6 per cent. It is true that the national average in Wales (59.8%) and England (55.3%) is much better than ours but Scotland (46.7%) and France (43.7%) are only just ahead of us. In many ways, Ireland's record speaks volumes for the standing of the game here.

The Irish Rugby Football Union was founded in Dublin in 1874 and, since it did not include Belfast, a different Union was formed North of the border. Yet when Ireland first played England at the Oval in 1875 there were Ulstermen present and four years later the rift was healed and the bodies joined together.

Ireland, boasting the second oldest club in the world, in Trinity College, experienced early difficulties and when they met England in that first game, without two of their best players, they lost by two goals and a try to nil.

Two years later they met Scotland for the first time, at the first international played in Belfast, and it was a rather forgettable experience from the Irish point of view, for they lost the game by six goals and two tries to nothing. These results — or losses — were to haunt Ireland in their play against both England and Scotland for the remainder of the century.

It should be remembered that since 1900, Ireland's record against both countries has improved dramatically from those early times. In the first 23 games against England and 22 against Scotland, Ireland managed only nine wins. I referred earlier to their overall record against each. Discount the period before 1900 and the average swells to 43.7 per cent against England and 57.7 per cent against Scotland. Our record against Wales has not really changed since the early years, for the 14 matches between 1882 and 1900 were evenly balanced. Only France and the Welsh can say they have gained ground against the Irish in recent years.

Statistics are all very well, but there is more to the Irish game than that. It is generally acknowledged that the Irish have a feel for the game. Something draws them to the excitement of the international arena and something in their nature spurs them to overcome difficult obstacles. All over the world, in national or Lions' jerseys, the Irish have won great respect.

Tom Kiernan played for his country 54 times. He captained the Irish team and the Lions, he coached Munster to an historic win over the All Blacks in 1980, and two seasons ago, with Ciaran Fitzgerald and 17 other highly charged men, helped plot a course towards a first Triple Crown triumph in 33 years, while also being in charge of the side which shared the championship last season.

Kiernan knows quite well the problems of the game here. He says:

> Because of the small numbers, it is difficult to produce good teams consistently, but yet I believe we produce players with better basic qualities than any of the others. Irish sportsmen in general are more realistic and honest and they have a better attitude. They play for the right reasons — for enjoyment — and they are, to my mind, more loyal than any of the other nations.

All countries, of course, produce rugby stars and characters who become known world-wide, some of whom become legends — men like Louis Magee, "Blucher" Doran, the Ryan brothers, Mick and Jack, Mossy Landers, Jammy Clinch, Eugene Davy, Jack Kyle, Karl Mullen, J. C. Daly, Tom Clifford, Tony O'Reilly, Ronnie Dawson, Dave Hewitt, Bill Mulcahy, Noel Murphy, Jerry Walsh, Tom Kiernan, Mike Gibson, Syd Millar, Willie John McBride, Fergus Slattery, Willie Duggan, Moss Keane and Ollie Campbell. There were, are, and will be many more.

One such legend surrounds Ernie Crawford, the man credited with inventing the world "Alickadoo". The term evidently originated when Crawford got annoyed with a colleague for being more interested in reading a book about the Orient than in joining a card game. Crawford snarled angrily at him: "Bloody Ali Khadu!" Subsequently, anyone who did not match up to Crawford's expectations was similarly christened, and today the word "Alickadoo" is commonly used to describe the non-playing members of clubs, men whose functions may or may not be defined.

The late Jammie Clinch was another of the old brigade. I met him only once, at an Irish squad training session a few years ago and he made no secret of the admiration he had for the current players, whom, he conceded, devoted much more time to training and to the finer points of the game than did he and his colleagues. But he was critical too and I recall one of his appearances when he fingered a player who had evidently shirked a tackle during the course of an international. This, to Clinch, was unforgivable. In *The Men of Green,* a book written in 1973 by my colleague, Sean Diffley *(Irish Independent),* Clinch of the twenties is described as having been "large, exuberant, fun-loving and not overly enamoured with following any pre-conceived policies." Diffley adds: "Crawford's approach was that of the Scarlet Pimpernel, circumventing difficulties by out-witting the other fellow. Jammie disdained all such niceties. He didn't hold at all with going around an obstacle, defini-tely preferring to go right through it".

Clinch built for himself quite a reputation, reflected,

perhaps, in the attitude of a Welsh fan who, on seeing the Irishman run onto the pitch before a match in Cardiff, screamed at the top of his voice: "Send the bastard off, ref!"

One of the great exponents of ball control on the ground — the dribble — was Tom Clifford. Described by Tony O'Reilly, in the Foreword, as a homely type, Clifford made a lasting impression on the other nationalities when selected for the 1950 Lions' tour to New Zealand. It is in a way a measure of the innocence of those times that before his departure his mother baked a number of large cakes for him to eat during the long voyage, thinking her son would be hungry. It is a measure of the way in which these stories gather momentum that his colleagues still say today that he had a special ship following the ocean liner to carry all the food he brought with him!

Stories about O'Reilly himself are endless. His endeavours for the Lions are well documented: 16 tries in South Africa in 1955 (a record), 17 in New Zealand in 1959 (a record he shares with John Bevan who achieved that number in 1971) and 5 more in Australia on the same tour. From the scoring point of view, he had less success for Ireland, probably because he was always a marked man, and possibly because of his recurring shoulder injury which hampered him at various stages of his career. Left out in the "cold" after 1963, O'Reilly set about building an international reputation as a businessman; by 1970 amongst other things he had worked his way up to a vice-presidentship of Heinz. That year, Ireland met England in Twickenham and after winger Bill Brown had cried off the team, O'Reilly was called upon as a shock replacement. He arrived at the match in a manner befitting his business status and found a telegram awaiting him from Johnny Quirke: "Heinz Beanz are Haz Beanz". O'Reilly recalls emerging from a ruck late in the game, after receiving a kick. Suddenly he heard a loud voice booming out, "And kick his chauffeur while you're there". This story is now recounted all over the world.

In 1974, Willie John McBride led the Lions in South

Africa and helped them to a famous series victory, documented later in this book. McBride, a well-known "wrecker" in his day, but now the exemplary captain, was still ready for a challenge to the witty side of his nature. There had, admits McBride, been a little misbehaviour by some of the players in one of the team hotels one evening: "Ah, there was some messing going on in a corridor. Someone had spilled drink and someone else had a fire hose or something."

Apparently the manager of the hotel, being rather unimpressed by the goings-on, challenged the culprits and warned them to behave. The answers he got were less than satisfactory and so he stormed off, threatening to call the police. At that very moment, McBride stepped from the lift; the manager stopped in his tracks and informed McBride of the incidents and of his intentions. "I vill call the police," he screamed. McBride looked stunned for a moment, then turned and asked: "And tell me, sir, how many of them will there be?"

Moss Keane may have learned some of the tricks of the trade from McBride when he packed down with him 10 times for Ireland in 1974 and 1975. But Keane certainly did not need any lessons in comedy. A big bustling Kerryman who knows not his own strength — and more than one Irish rugby journalist can testify to that — Moss has a tendency to open buttons of other people's shirts rather hastily, yet he possesses a droll, infinite sense of humour.

Elsewhere is documented his fear of flying and his cure for that problem. How can one ever forget the look of absolute horror on his face as he watched the captain of a Romanian turbo prop aircraft circle the plane and then kick the tyres to check for pressure? How can one forget the subsequent illogical dialogue between a Romanian aircraft captain and an Irish Agricultural Inspector while Keane sought desperately to find out "what the bloody hell" was going on?

There is the tale, too, of his vain attempt to score a try against France at Lansdowne Road last season. Moss emerged from a ruck and charged towards the French line. Just as he was about to get the touch-down, a French player hit him from the side and the ball popped agonisingly away from him. That is the fact of the matter. But later, in seeking to capitalise on the issue, Moss claimed that he had done it deliberately: "Well, it was like this: I was over the line when all of a sudden I remembered that McBride had scored against France in his last international at Lansdowne Road. To score might have meant the end of my career, so I decided I'd better not!"

Fergus Slattery, Ireland's long-serving flanker, has been around long enough to build up a dossier of stories on the players he has soldiered with through the years, but one favourite of his concerns Willie Duggan when he was in South Africa a few years ago. Duggan was playing in an exhibition match and had not been exactly setting the world alight. Finally he came off the pitch in a state of near exhaustion, taking to a bench near the sideline. When another player was tackled into touch, he noticed Willie grinding his heel into the ground. Curious, he asked him what he was doing. "This damn snail has been following me around all afternoon and I've finally caught up with him," came the tongue-in-cheek reply.

The list of stories and anecdotes about legendary rugby figures is endless.

Ireland's competitive edge over the years has not been blunt, even if success in the Triple Crown and the championship has been hard to secure. The Triple Crown win in 1982 bridged a 33-year gap and it was only our fifth such win, the others coming in 1894, 1899, 1948 and 1949. It was also our ninth outright championship win (we have shared it seven times), but the Grand Slam, which we won for the only time in 1948, eluded us.

One of the English players defeated by Ireland at Lansdowne Road last season confessed: "I wish we had the same attitude. We could have played them 100 times last year and we would have lost 99. There was a defeatist attitude in our side, sad to relate."

Obviously that happens to every team, but if the Irish collapse from time to time on the field, no matter what happens they attempt to meet the challenge. The Irish revel in the role of "underdog" and very often in that situation defy the critics.

Great progress has been made in the game over the last couple of decades and skills have improved with the advent of coaching, even if, like the other home countries, back play seems to have suffered. That problem has been identified, yet it is a matter of urgency that the coaches begin to do something about it.

Interest is growing all the time in rugby. Towns which heretofore were strongholds of other sports, notably GAA, have now begun to take a serious interest in the game. Rugby will never be the major interest in these areas. It will never rival Gaelic games in terms of playing numbers, but the time is ripe for a certain amount of change and the rugby authorities must ensure that youngsters being introduced into the code are given every opportunity for proper coaching.

The future of Irish rugby? Tom Kiernan could not offer a definite answer to that, but he said:

> Ireland's destiny is in its own hands. The chances of staying at the top on a consistent basis are pretty slim unless we work much harder than other countries. We have to get it right in the schools' and youths' sections, in the clubs, at provincial and selectorial levels. That is where we must prepare the platform. We are involved in international competition against bigger nations. We must not expect, nor will we get, any sympathy if we fail to compete with them successfully.

CHAPTER 3

THE EARLY YEARS

Although the English were the touring pioneers, well before the dawning of the 20th century Ireland had made a handsome contribution to the success of overseas tours.

It would be correct to point out that the first tour – to Australia and New Zealand in 1888 – had the backing of, but was not instigated by, the Rugby Football Union, and indeed many of the players included were not Union players, or did not later gain international honours.

There were no Irishmen in that first touring party, led by Englishman R. L. Seddon, who was soon to die tragically in a boating accident. The death was an obvious blow to the members of the party, but it did not affect their play. With A. E. Stoddard, one of the initiators of the tour, taking over the captaincy, they returned home in triumph, having gained 27 victories and six draws. They lost only two games – to Auckland and Taranaki on the New Zealand sector of the trip.

1891: SOUTH AFRICA

Three years later, in 1891, another touring party left Britain. This time the Rugby Union were fully behind it. The challenge had come from South Africa and had to be met. And indeed it was superbly met, for in all 19 matches the British tourists emerged victorious. Theirs was a remarkable record: they conceded just one point in their opening game against Cape Town clubs and kept a clean sheet thereafter. They rattled up a points tally of 223 and "whitewashed" South Africa in the test series.

1888 RESULTS

Played	Won	Drew	Lost	For	Against
35	27	6	2	300	101

Otago	W	8-3
Otago	W	4-3
Canterbury	W	14-6
Canterbury	W	4-0
Wellington	D	3-3
Roberts XV	W	4-1*
Taranaki Clubs	L	0-1*
Auckland	W	6-3
Auckland	L	0-4
New South Wales	W	18-2
Bathurst	W	13-6
New South Wales	W	18-6
Sydney Juniors	W	11-0
King's School, Sydney	D	10-10
Sydney Grammar	D	3-3
Bathurst	W	20-10
New South Wales	W	16-2
University of Sydney	W	8-4
Newcastle	W	15-7
Queensland	W	13-6
Queensland Juniors	W	11-3
Queensland	W	7-0
Ipswich	W	12-1*
Melbourne	W	15-5
Adelaide	W	28-3
Auckland	W	3-0
Auckland	D	1-1*
Hawkes Bay	W	3-2

Played	Won	Drew	Lost	For	Against
35	27	6	2	300	101

Wairarapa	W	5-1*
Canterbury	W	8-0
Otago	D	0-0
South Island	W	5-3
South Island	W	6-0
Taranaki Clubs	W	7-1*
Wanganui	D	1-1*

* Try = 1 point

Played	Won	Drew	Lost	For	Against
19	19	0	0	223	1

Cape Town Clubs	W 15-1*
Western Province	W 6-0
Cape Colony	W 14-0
Kimberly	W 7-0
Griqualand West	W 3-0
Port Elisabeth	W 22-0
Eastern Province	W 21-0
SOUTH AFRICA	W 4-0
Grahamstown District	W 9-0
King Williams Town	W 18-0
King Williams Town and District	W 15-0
Natal	W 25-0
Transvaal	W 22-0
Johannesburg	W 15-0
Johannesburg/Pretoria	W 9-0
Cape Colony	W 4-0
SOUTH AFRICA	W 3-0
Cape Colony	W 7-0
SOUTH AFRICA	W 4-0

*Try = 1 point

At last! 1896 was the year of the Irish in every sense. One might have excused Irish rugby players of the time for thinking they were being ignored. But their destiny lay in their own hands.

Two years before, Ireland had won the Triple Crown for the first time, and the man to the forefront of their successful challenge was Tommy Crean of Wanderers. Crean was to become famous in more than one sphere of life later on.

Scotland took the Triple Crown in 1895 and after that, fears were expressed that Ireland might have to wait longer for representation on a touring side. But back they came to win the 1896 championship and they did it in such style that they were to have the biggest representation of all the countries when the touring party for South Africa was announced.

Nine of the 21 players were Irish and although an Englishman, John Hammond, was named as captain, Tommy Crean was to have a profound influence on the tour, leading the side in two of the test matches and several of the provincial games. Crean was quite a character by all accounts, both on and off the pitch, and, along, with his Irish colleagues, did more than any other nationality for the success of the tour.

Crean received lavish praise in the journals of the time. South African critics were amazed that a man of his size (he stood 6 feet 2 inches) could be so mobile. What they did not know was that Crean was a sprint champion who, above all, liked to run. When in full flight he was almost impossible to stop, for his speed, strength and high knee action combined made him one of the toughest players of his day. By the end of the tour, Crean had contributed five tries, made many more and built for himself an enviable reputation as a leader of men. It was no surprise then that such a superb footballer and instigator should go on to show his bravery elsewhere.

In the early tours, it was not uncommon for players to

remain on in the countries which they toured. So it was for Crean, and a fellow clubman, Robert Johnston. They took advantage of the "assisted" passage and when the Boer War broke out in 1899, both joined the Imperial Light Horse, an army unit set up in the Transvaal.

Crean worked his way up to the rank of captain and was wounded while helping his unit defend their position at Tygerskloof. He continued on in his characteristic fashion to help his fellow soldiers and when struck again, he was said to have called out: "By Christ, I'm killed entirely." However, Crean did not die. For his bravery he was awarded the Victoria Cross. He went on to fight in World War 1, winning another medal for bravery, and later settled down to practice as a doctor in Harley Street.

Crean's colleague, Johnston, did not make as big a name for himself on the playing pitches. He had been capped just twice for Ireland and although reasonably successful in South Africa, did not win his place on the test sides. In battle, however, he was just as valiant. Some months before Crean's day of glory, Johnston helped his unit — he was also a captain in the Imperial Light Horse — to a great victory against tremendous odds. He displayed courage beyond that normally exercised, and for his bravery he, too, was awarded the prized Victoria Cross.

Louis Magee had, the season before, established himself as a half-back of note on the Irish team. He was to go on to become one of the most fêted Irish internationals of all time. He eventually played 28 times for his country, but far away from home, in that summer of 1896, he was soon winning himself a new band of admirers. He was joined on the tour by his brother, J. T. Magee, who played in the same side at Bective Rangers. J. T., an international cricketer, never actually played rugby for Ireland. But in South Africa he played impressively and got two outings in tests. impressively and got two outings in tests.

Another interesting personality on the 1896 tour was A. D. Clinch, who played ten times in all for his country. He was the father of a future international of note, Jammie

Clinch, one of the great characters of the game.

Universities rugby was very strong in those days and it was no real surprise that four men from Dublin University should have been included in the touring party. L. Q. Bulger, J. Sealy, A. D. Meares and C. A. Boyd were the quartet, and if Bulger and Sealy were the more successful players on that tour, then the experience gained in South Africa helped mould the other two into great future international players. Boyd finally won three caps, in 1900 and 1901, while Meares played four times in 1899 and 1900.

Sealy played for Ireland nine times between 1896 and 1900 and, like Bulger, who won eight caps for Ireland, played in all four tests on tour. Bulger was undoubtedly the most prolific try-getter. Altogether he scored 20 tries, which represented over 30 per cent of the tourists' total of 65.

And so it was that nine Irishmen forged their first links with a team which was later to become the British and Irish Lions.

Played	Won	Drew	Lost	For	Against
21	19	1	1	320	45

Capetown clubs	W 14-9
Suburban Clubs	W 8-0
Western Province	D 0-0
Griqualand West	W 11-9
Griqualand West	W 16-0
Port Elizabeth/Uitenhage	W 26-3
Eastern Province	W 18-0
SOUTH AFRICA	W 8-0
Grahamstown	W 20-0
King Williams Town	W 25-0
East London	W 27-0
Queenstown	W 25-0
Johannesburg/Country	W 7-0
Transvaal	W 16-3
Johannesburg/Town	W 18-0
Transvaal	W 16-5
SOUTH AFRICA	W 17-8
Cape Colony	W 7-0
SOUTH AFRICA	W 9-3
Western Province	W 32-0
SOUTH AFRICA	L 0-5

Tom McGown had the distinction of becoming the first player from a Northern Ireland club to tour abroad with a British and Irish side. He was one of three Irishmen selected on the team to tour Australia, a trip which remains unique in the history of the Lions. It was the first and last time that a British Isles side travelled to that country without also visiting New Zealand.

The records of that particular tour are rather scant, but it seems strange that only McGown (NIFC), E. Martelli (Dublin University) and G. P. Doran (Lansdowne) made the trip from Ireland, particularly as Ireland had dominated the home internationals that season.

They won the Triple Crown for the second time and both Doran and McGown helped them do it. Martelli seemed to have come from nowhere — another of the players in those early days who never won a cap for their own country, but yet toured abroad.

Doran was to go on to a distinguished international career, winning a respectable eight caps, while McGown, though not faring as well, played three times for his country.

Played	Won	Drew	Lost	For	Against
21	18	0	3	333	90

Central Southern	W 11-3
New South Wales	W 4-3
Metropolitan	W 8-5
AUSTRALIA	L 3-13
Toowoomba	W 19-5
Queensland	L 3-11
Bundaberg	W 36-3
Rockhampton	W 16-3
Mount Morgan	W 29-3
Central Queensland	W 22-3
Maryborough	W 27-8
AUSTRALIA	W 11-0
New England	W 6-4
Northern	W 28-0
New South Wales	W 11-5
Metropolitan	L 5-8
Western	W 19-0
AUSTRALIA	W 13-0
Schools	W 21-3
Victoria	W 30-0
AUSTRALIA	W 11-10

I. G. Davidson (NIFC) and Hugh Ferris (Queen's University, Belfast) played together for Ireland three times — against Scotland and Wales in 1900 and against Wales in 1901.

How ironic it would have been then, had these two fellow-countrymen been drawn in opposition when yet another British/Irish team travelled to South Africa in 1903; for Ferris, who had played altogether four times for Ireland, was set to line out for his adopted country, South Africa, to which he had emigrated the previous year.

The confrontation was not to be, for while Davidson played in the first test match which ended in a 10-10 draw, he failed to win a place in the remaining two internationals. Ferris, by all accounts, made a handsome contribution for the home side on that September day in 1903, helping them to an 8-0 victory and to the series. The second game had also been drawn.

Davidson was one of five Irishmen on that particular tour and the only back, but while this was the worst trip by a British side up to then, the Irish were certainly not to blame. They provided four of the 11 forwards, and each of them — A. D. Tedford (Malone), R. S. Smyth (Dublin University) and brothers Joseph and James Wallace (Wanderers) — distinguished themselves.

It was perhaps time that Ireland should produce another forward in the mould of Tommy Crean, and they did, in A. D. Tedford. Tedford was highly regarded by the South Africans and assessed as a marvellous scrummager and runner. Small in stature, he made up for that with pace, stamina and anticipation. A most durable player, he played in all three tests and eventually won 23 caps for Ireland.

James Wallace was uncapped when embarking on the trip but made such an impression that he played in two of the internationals, before returning home to win two Irish caps in 1904. His brother, Joseph, had an international career spanning four seasons and won a total of ten caps, playing in one test in South Africa. The fourth Irish forward was R. S. Smith, who played in all the test sides on tour and scored one try.

But even the best efforts of the Irish could not deny South Africa revenge this time. It was a very strong British Isles side, but yet they lost the first three matches — all against different Western Province teams. They had a run of five wins, then lost three more in a row. Their last provincial defeat came against Transvaal; they drew the first two tests but lost the series when they were defeated in the last test in Cape Town.

Played	Won	Drew	Lost	For	Against
22	11	3	8	229	138

Western Province (Country)	L	7-13
Western Province (Town)	L	3-12
Western Province	L	4-8
Port Elizabeth	W	13-0
Eastern Province	W	12-0
Grahamstown	W	28-7
King Williams Town	W	37-3
East London	W	7-5
Griqualand West	L	0-11
Griqualand West	L	6-8
Transvaal	L	3-12
Pretoria	W	15-3
Petermaritzburg	W	15-0
Durban	W	22-0
Witwatersrand	W	12-0
Transvaal	L	4-14
SOUTH AFRICA	D	10-10
Orange River Colony	W	17-16
Griqualand West	W	11-5
SOUTH AFRICA	D	0-0
Western Province	D	3-3
SOUTH AFRICA	L	0-8

The name O'Brien would seem to suggest an Irish background, but although Guy's Hospital player, A. B. O'Brien, was probably Irish, this is not documented in accounts of the visit to Australia and New Zealand in 1904.

There was a distinct absence of established international players on this tour, which followed so closely on the heels of the trip to South Africa. While we can only wonder about the background of the said A. B. O'Brien, who, in addition to being a playing member, was also manager, there were three bona fide Irishmen in the party.

One was C. D. Patterson, a forward from Malone, but he was uncapped at the time and indeed never made the Irish team afterwards either. Another was his club colleague, R. W. Edwards, who evidently did much to ensure the success of the tour. They won all their matches in Australia and had a fifty per cent record in New Zealand, although they lost the only test there by nine points to three. Edwards made that test side and was evidently one of the greatest supports for the captain, D. R. (Darky) Bedell-Sivright, who was capped 22 times for Scotland between 1900 and 1908 and who had won "Blues" for Cambridge University in 1899, 1900, 1901 and 1902. The remaining Irishman was B. S. Massey who played for Ulster but was never capped for Ireland, although he did play one test match against Australia.

Played	Won	Drew	Lost	For	Against
19	16	1	2	287	84

New South Wales	W 27-0
Combined Western Districts	W 21-6
New South Wales	W 29-6
Metropolitan Union	W 19-6
AUSTRALIA	W 17-0
Northern Districts	W 17-3
Queensland	W 24-5
Metropolitan Union	W 17-3
Queensland	W 18-7
Toowoomba	W 12-3
AUSTRALIA	W 17-3
New South Wales	W 5-0
New England	W 26-9
AUSTRALIA	W 16-0
South Canterbury/Canterbury/West Coast	W 5-3
Otago/Southland	W 14-8
NEW ZEALAND	L 3-9
Taranaki/Wanganui/Manawatu	D 0-0
Auckland	L 0-13

CHAPTER 4

A CAPTAIN AT LAST

Ireland's long wait for a leader of an overseas tour ended in 1910, when Dr Tom Smyth of Malone and Newport was given the honour of heading a party of 30 players on a 24-match trip to South Africa.

This was the first official representation of the four home unions and Smyth's fine performance for Ireland in the three preceding seasons suggested that he was the ideal man for the job. Certainly, all accounts of the tour confirm that he was an excellent leader, even if the results did not always favour his side.

In fact they were rather inconsistent; while the party won 13 games, they lost another eight and drew three. South Africa won two of the three internationals, despite the best efforts of Smyth and the "man of the tour", young Englishman, "Cherry" Pillman. The latter started out as a wing-forward, but played in the second test at out-half, helping his side to an eight points to three victory.

Smyth won a total of 14 caps for his country between 1908 and 1912 and was the most experienced Irishman on this tour.

But another Northern Ireland man, A. R. Foster of Derry, who had only just sprung to international prominence, was to emulate him, winning 17 caps altogether, the final one in 1921. Foster was one of six Irishmen in South Africa in 1910 and finished as second top try-scorer, after England's M. E. Neale.

Smyth and Foster were joined by two more Northern Ireland players: W. Tyrrell, a student at Queen's University, Belfast, and A. N. McClinton (NIFC). Tyrrell had come into the Irish team before the touring party departed for South Africa and although he did not play in the test side, he had a good tour. He later went on to win 9 caps for his country. McClinton had played against Wales and France that year but on tour did not play well enough to get in for the internationals.

The news that two Cork men — O. J. S. Piper (Constitution) and W. J. Ashby (Queen's College Cork) — had been included was joyously welcomed in the Southern capital for they became the first players from the city to be so honoured. Ashby was uncapped at the time and did not make a great impression, but the established international, Piper, had a marvellous tour, playing in the first test when the visiting side went down by 14 points to 10.

So, despite some poor results, history at least was made with the elevation of Tom Smyth to captain. And if the tour was, overall, a disappointing one, it set a precedent, for many more Irishmen were to be singled out for a similar honour.

Played	Won	Drew	Lost	For	Against
26	16	1	9	323	201

1910 RESULTS

Played	Won	Drew	Lost	For	Against
24	13	3	8	290	226

South-West Districts	W 14-4
Western Provinces (Country)	W 9-3
Western Provinces (College)	W 11-3
Western Provinces (Town)	D 11-11
Western Province	W 5-3
Griqualand West	L 0-8
Transvaal	L 8-27
Pretoria	W 17-0
Transvaal (Country)	W 45-4
Transvaal	L 6-13
Natal	W 18-16
Natal	W 19-13
Orange River Colony	W 12-9
Griqualand West	L 3-9
Cape Colony	L 0-19
Rhodesia	W 24-11
SOUTH AFRICA	L 10-14
North-East Districts	D 8-8
Border	W 30-10
Border	W 13-13
Eastern Province	W 14-6
SOUTH AFRICA	W 8-3
SOUTH AFRICA	L 5-21
Western Province	L 0-8

When Lansdowne and Irish half-back, W. Cunningham, left the shores of Ireland in 1923, bound for a new life in South Africa, little did he know that within months he would be joining forces with former colleagues against friends in his new homeland. Rather the opposite of the situation which faced Hugh Ferris 21 years earlier.

This British and Irish side, which at this time was generally referred to as "The Lions", had severe injury problems, so much so, that before the first test, one of the three quarters had to be drafted into the pack in order to make up the eight. The introduction of Cunningham, then, came directly as a result of injury to key players, but that is not to say that he did not contribute. He certainly did.

Capped by Ireland eight times between 1920 and 1923, Cunningham seemed set for a long international career before he decided to emigrate. While the Lions did not have a happy tour results-wise — they lost nine and drew three of their 21 games — Cunningham scored a magnificent try in the third test which was the only one of the four in which the tourists managed to avoid defeat. Cunningham, the reserve, was the only Irish back to have taken part, and it was a strange quirk of fate that he should have been responsible for their best international performance.

The 1924 pack was strong and tough, and played hard. It included a man who had only that season burst onto the Irish scene: J. M. McVicker of Collegians, who appeared in three of the tests and then went on to a most distinguished career in the Irish jersey, winning a total of 20 caps by 1930.

It also included Jammie Clinch (Dublin University and Wanderers), whose fame spread throughout the rugby world within a short time of his return from South Africa. When he travelled on that tour, he had not really established himself on the Irish side, although he had won five caps. He did not make the test teams but returned home having obviously learned a great deal from his experience, for he spent a further seven seasons representing Ireland and finally won 30 caps.

Clinch was as colourful a character as any of the greats who went before him. A man who liked individuality, he was also a dedicated team player and was one of the toughest men ever to don the Irish jersey. He apparently got his nickname, Jammie, because he was said to have devoted a lot of time to making jam sandwiches in school, when his attentions might better have been given to books. That name was to follow him through life and, indeed, up to his death a few years ago he was well known for his appearances on RTE sports programmes, when he would analyse the Irish rugby teams and the problems they were facing then. At times, it seemed, he was less than kind to some players of the present day, but one feels sure he would have been more than happy to have seen Ireland winning their fifth Triple Crown in 1982.

T. N. Brand (NIFC) was uncapped when selected for the tour and although on his return he played once for Irleand, when they lost 6-0 to New Zealand, he was never to play at that level again. However, he did well in South Africa in 1924, so well, in fact, that he was included in two of the tests and, according to the records available, his overall contribution was a handsome one.

Dolphin's M. J. Bradley was a famous Irish forward of the 1920s and in both 1926 and 1927 he helped Ireland to a share in the international championship with Scotland. In all he was capped 19 times and if he did not play at international level, he was reckoned to be a good Lions tourist.

Newport created something of a record in the 1910 tour, when they had more representatives than any other club. They continued that trend in 1924 by having four of their men included. One of these was Dr W. J. Roche, who had won three caps for Ireland in 1920. Roche was a Corkman and had played for his country while he was a student at University College, Cork.

Played	Won	Drew	Lost	For	Against
21	9	3	9	175	155

Western Province (Town and Country)	L	6-7
Western Province (Universities)	W	9-8
Griqualand West	W	26-0
Rhodesia	W	16-3
Western Transvaal	W	8-7
Transvaal	D	12-12
Orange Free State (Country)	L	0-6
Orange Free State	L	3-6
Natal	D	3-3
SOUTH AFRICA	L	3-7
Witwatersrand	L	6-10
SOUTH AFRICA	L	0-17
Pretoria	L	0-6
Cape Colony	W	13-3
North-East Districts	W	20-12
Border	W	12-3
Eastern Province	L	6-14
SOUTH AFRICA	D	3-3
South-West Districts	W	12-6
SOUTH AFRICA	L	9-16
Western Province	W	8-6

More than 20 years after the Anglo-Welsh tour to New Zealand, the 1930 British Isles side set out for further combat with the "All Blacks". It was a trip that took them not just to New Zealand, but also to Australia, and they finished with a tour record of 20 wins and eight losses.

It might well have become known as the "Baggy Pants" tour, for the visitors were clad in rather clumsy-looking shorts, sporting large pockets to keep their hands warm during periods of inactivity (if any).

Yet while they lost the test series 1-3, having had an encouraging start, it was a fairly successful undertaking and their points tally of 624 was the biggest to date.

In keeping with the new tradition, there was a fair sprinkling of Irish blood in the party. Five players in all from Ireland made the trip: P. F. Murray (Wanderers), the only back, G. R. (George) Beamish (Leicester), M. J. Dunne (Lansdowne), J. L. Farrell (Bective) and H. O'H. O'Neill (Queen's University).

Beamish was the most experienced of the Irish players and was regarded as one of the best foreign forwards ever seen in New Zealand. Naturally enough then, with several Irish caps behind him and more to come (25 in all), he played a major role in making the tour, despite the test disappointments, a reasonably good one, particularly from the scoring point of view. He played in all the tests.

J. L. Farrell was another of the stalwarts. He played 29 times altogether for Ireland, first in 1926, and like Beamish, he appeared in all of the tests. So too did H. O'H. O'Neill, who sprang to prominence with Queen's University, but who later moved to University College, Cork, to further his studies.

P. F. Murray of Wanderers played in three tests in New Zealand and the one in Australia. His play on the tour was generally very satisfactory; and if M. J. Dunne was the only one of the five not to have won a test place he went on to wear the Irish jersey 16 times before his retirement in 1934.

48

Played	Won	Drew	Lost	For	Against
28	20	0	8	624	318

Wanganui	W 19-3
Taranaki	W 23-7
Manawhenua	W 34-8
Wairarapa & Bush	W 19-6
Wellington	L 8-12
Canterbury	L 8-14
Buller/West Coast	W 34-11
Otago	W 33-9
NEW ZEALAND	W 6-3
Southland	W 9-3
Ashburton/South Canterbury/ North Otago	W 16-9
NEW ZEALAND	L 10-13
Maoris	W 19-13
Hawkes Bay	W 14-3
East Coast/Poverty Bay/Bay of Plenty	W 25-11
Auckland	L 6-19
NEW ZEALAND	L 10-15
North Auckland	W 38-5
Waikato/Thames Valley/King Country	W 40-16
NEW ZEALAND	L 8-22
Marlborough/Nelson & Golden Bay	W 41-3
New South Wales	W 29-10
AUSTRALIA	L 5-6
Queensland	W 26-16
Australian XV	W 29-14
New South Wales	L 3-28
Victoria	W 41-36
Western Australia (unofficial)	W 71-3

CHAPTER 5

FOUR IN A ROW

Belfast prop forward, Sammy Walker, became the second Irish captain of the Lions when he led a party of 29 players, eight of them Irish, to South Africa in 1938.

It might never have happened, for Walker, while playing rugby in school, was said to have preferred Association Football, often incurring the wrath of games masters for pursuing his interest in that code. Later in his life, however, it became quite apparent that his future lay in rugby. He was tough, he was strong, and his reputation as a superb scrummager helped win him a place on the Irish team in 1934, after a few seasons of great displays for his club, Instonians, and for his province, Ulster.

The 1938 Lions will not be remembered for a series win, because quite simply they failed. But they will never be forgotten for an unlikely, quite sensational, victory in the final test which saved a "whitewash". Sammy Walker and the remainder of the Irish contingent all took part in that famous victory. The fact that eight Irishmen were on that side is quite unique. It never happened before, and the chances of it happening again are remote.

It should be pointed out that this side was riddled with injury in South Africa, which probably accounted for the large Irish representation in the final test. Nevertheless, the inclusion of so many Irish players was to prove highly rewarding.

The Lions had been beaten fairly badly in the two preceding internationals by a Danie Craven-inspired South African side, the bulk of whom had undertaken a successful tour to Australia and New Zealand some months before. In those first tests the South Africans scored 45 points to the Lions' combined total of 15. They had scored seven tries as against one by the Lions.

It seemed as though the scene was set for a dismal end for Sammy Walker and his party. The signs looked even more ominous at half-time, when the Lions trailed by ten points on a 13-3 scoreline.

But Walker had other ideas; within two minutes of the resumption of play, he inspired the comeback, sending in Englishman G. T. Dancer for the try after a fine break. Harry McKibbin added the points and then kicked a penalty to put them within sight of victory, before another Irishman, Bob Alexander, gave them the lead with a great try, set up for him by George Cromey (Queen's University).

The Springboks went back in front with a penalty but Scottish full-back G. F. Grieve, deputising for the injured Vivian Jenkins (Wales), dropped a goal — worth four points — and his compatriot, P. L. Duff, sealed it with a try before the end: 21-16 to the Lions!

Thus Sammy Walker finished a happy international career on a winning note. He had played for Ireland on 15 occasions, but did not reappear for the one season left before the outbreak of World War II. C. R. A. Graves of Wanderers, who played in two of those tests, had a career remarkably similar to that of Walker, winning 15 caps beginning and ending in the same seasons as his colleague.

The remainder of the Irish contingent went on to appear for their country in 1939. C. V. Boyle (Dublin University), who also had two test appearances in South Africa, won a total of nine caps, the last against Wales in the following season. Harry McKibbin (Queen's University) had only one cap to his credit en route to the Southern hemisphere, but after three test outings and having scored 30 points on tour, he won three more caps for his country.

Undoubtedly the real character of the side was Queen's

University player Blair Mayne, who was one of the four Irishmen to have appeared in all three tests. Mayne was a tough forward in the mould of Tommy Crean, and he became yet another to distinguish himself in wartime, making his name in the Middle East with the Special Air Service. In all, Mayne played six times for his country — between 1937 and 1939.

Bob Alexander of NIFC was equally effective on the tour, scoring six tries, none more important than the crucial one in the third test. He won his first cap in 1936 and was a regular until 1939, appearing 11 times altogether.

The half-backs for that final test were George Cromey, the fifth of the Ulster men in the party, and G. J. Morgan (Clontarf). For both, it was their only appearance against the Springboks, and how well they took their chance! They combined magnificently together, and, like the rest of the side, covered themselves in glory. Cromey had come onto the Irish team in 1937 and played nine times between then and 1939. Morgan was there longer, having worked his way on back in 1934, and he won a total of 19 caps, the last in 1939.

Played	Won	Drew	Lost	For	Against
23	17	0	6	407	272

Border	W 11-8
Griqualand West	W 22-9
Western Province (Town & Country)	L 8-11
South-West Districts	W 19-10
Western Province	L 11-21
Western Transvaal	W 26-9
Orange Free State	W 21-6
Orange Free State (Country)	W 18-3
Transvaal	L 9-16
Northern Transvaal	W 20-12
Cape Province	W 10-3
Rhodesia	W 25-11
Rhodesia	W 45-11
Transvaal	W 17-9
SOUTH AFRICA	L 12-26
Northern Province	L 8-26
Natal	W 15-11
Border	W 19-11
North-East District	W 42-3
Eastern Province	W 6-5
SOUTH AFRICA	L 3-19
SOUTH AFRICA	W 21-16
Combined University	W 19-16
Western Province Country (unofficial)	L 7-12

When Karl Mullen was appointed captain of the Lions for their 1950 tour to New Zealand and Australia, it was another "first" in the history of the team's activities. For he was the first South of Ireland Catholic to lead representatives from Britain and Ireland overseas. The selectors seemed to have little doubt that Mullen, who led Ireland to Grand Slam and Triple Crown victories, would be the ideal captain, but they were still apprehensive. So much so that he was summoned to London.

Mullen recalls: "I think people were scared that I might have been a Fenian. I assured them of course that I was not, and promised there would be no politics."

It had been 20 years since the last Lions tour to those countries and on the playing front he was given the instruction to have his team run the ball at every opportunity. It was to be a "goodwill" tour, during which the Lions would show the very best of what British rugby had to offer and New Zealand would do the same.

Certainly New Zealand went through their paces, playing so well that they won the test series without the loss of a single match. But in a sense they broke their side of the bargain, for while Mullen's Lions were showing gay abandon in the use of their backs, the All Blacks were playing it tight, determined to win at all costs. And the shrewd use of a powerful pack, allied with a mundane but efficient backline, gave them the series.

Mullen admits: "If I had my way we might have played differently. Certainly we had many great backs and it would have been foolish not to use players like Jack Kyle, Bleddyn Williams, Jack Matthews and Ken Jones, but I was used to Irish rugby and that meant playing it tight. Here we were committed to the type of stuff which the Barbarians produce. It was very popular but I feel it cost us the series, or at least a share of the spoils."

However Mullen, who is now an eminent Dublin gynaecologist, was happy that Ireland's contribution to the Lions was recognised fully for the first time in 1950, when a new strip of red shirts, white shorts and blue stockings with a green fringe was devised. He may not have been satisfied with the test results but was extremely pleased with the Irish performances on tour. And Mullen was quite emphatic when he declared: "There would have been no tour without Jack Kyle".

His admiration knows no bounds for Ireland's legendary out-half, who was in "full flight" on this tour. Kyle teased and tantalised both Australia and New Zealand with a series of brilliant displays, all of which prompted even the most partisan of fans to declare he was the best they had ever seen. That opinion has been endorsed many times over. Kyle played in all the tests, and if he was only seventh in the list of top try-scorers with a total of seven, he contributed to many more. He graced the Irish jersey on 46 occasions altogether — a record for a fly-half — and his international career spanned 12 seasons.

Kyle was one of three Queen's University players on the tour; the other two were Noel Henderson and Bill McKay. Henderson, at 21 years of age, had three internationals behind him and because of that lack of experience was not expected to challenge Williams and Matthews in the centre. In the event, he could not break up the partnership, but his form was so good that he played in one test against the All Blacks — on the wing. He scored eight tries on tour and went on to a great career with Ireland, winning 40 caps by 1959.

Apart from the captain, Karl Mullen, and Kyle, perhaps the biggest Irish influence on the tour was flanker Bill McKay who played in all six tests. McKay is reckoned by many to be the greatest Irish flanker of all time and his displays in New Zealand in particular won him great praise. "His contribution was enormous. His fitness, determination and work rate was a spur to all of us", said Mullen, who recalled that having broken his nose, McKay was fitted with a special harness to protect his face, and he then lined out the following week in one of the test games.

McKay was another Irishman who distinguished himself in battle. During World War II he had joined the British Army and was one of the famous "Wingate Raiders" Commando unit. He was twice sent on missions behind Japanese lines in Burma and on one occasion was one of only a few dozen who returned.

Bill McKay enjoyed the tour to New Zealand, which established him as one of the great rugby characters. During that time he was studying medicine and before departing, he entrusted a medical book to the care of legendary Limerick forward, Tom Clifford. Several times during the tour Clifford proffered it, but each time McKay turned him down. He finally took back the book when the party arrived back in London, over six months later. That particular period of inactive study did not seem to hamper the wing-forward however for he did qualify as a doctor.

Jim Nelson (Malone) was the last of the Northern Ireland contingent and his value as a tight forward, and a good ball handler and dribbler was displayed several times on tour. Nelson is now one of the top administrators in the game, having in 1982 completed a year as President of the Irish Rugby Football Union. On the 1950 tour he played in four tests — two in New Zealand and two in Australia. A member of the triumphant Irish teams in 1948 and 1949, his international career began in 1947 and ended in 1954, during which period he won a total of 16 caps.

The tour ended almost before it began for Bective's George Norton who broke his arm early on . . . and thereby hangs a tale. There has always been a great deal of controversy about the New Zealand attitude to players lying on the ball. Unwittingly or otherwise, Norton "transgressed" and suffered the consequences — a broken arm — which brought to an end his influence on the playing side of the tour. Mullen's reaction? "Their attitude was different to ours and I suppose in a way they had a point on the law. They made no apologies for the incident. In their view he should not have been there."

In any event, the incident seemed to have little effect on

Norton's enjoyment of the tour off the pitch. He was, by all accounts, a witty and likeable character and one story from Mullen sums him up.

The captain was always conscious of the behaviour of his players. This, after all, was a goodwill tour, and as leader he was responsible for their actions off the park. On leaving one particular hotel after a four-day stay, he was approached by the manager. "Here goes," said Mullen to himself, "What have they done?"

Earlier in the week the players had been supplied with crates of Guinness and for some "unknown" reason the crates had also been packed with straw. Mullen was surprised by the mild behaviour of the manager, who proceeded to thank him profusely, but then the question was posed: "Would you please tell me how did the horse get into room 406?" It transpired that George Norton was registered in that room, although, admitted Mullen, "One cannot say he was responsible!"

It was not quite a great tour as far as Jim McCarthy (Dolphin) was concerned. McCarthy had a brilliant career for Ireland, lasting from 1948 to 1955, but his style was not suited to New Zealand rugby and so, although acquitting himself excellently in several provincial games, he failed to make the test series. He did, however, score four fine tries.

McCarthy's Cork colleague, Mick Lane of UCC, who was first capped in 1947, and who had shared in the Triple Crown victory of 1949 with him, fared better. Lane played a test match in each of the countries and scored a total of four tries on tour. By the end of his international career in 1953, he had won 17 caps for Ireland.

When Tom Clifford arrived home to Limerick after his lengthy trip, a crowd of almost 8,000 took to the streets to welcome him. Marching bands appeared on virtually every street corner and the Young Munster prop forward, who had brought fame to his club and city, was fêted lavishly. He deserved it, for after all, he was the first member of a Shannonside club to be selected for the Lions.

Clifford had a brilliant tour, according to Mullen, and his performances in Zew Zealand and Australia are well documented. He played in five of the six tests and if one outstanding forward had to be chosen, then Clifford was strongly challenging McKay for that honour.

Off the pitch, Clifford was equally popular and many funny stories have been told about him. Like the occasion when he scared Karl Mullen by saying he would refuse to stand for the British National Anthem. Like the time he marched behind a brass band in Nelson, insisting they had turned out only for him.

A genial character, Clifford, however, took some things seriously, and food was one of them. Renowned for his prowess at the dinner table, he went through the entire menu consisting of 18 courses one evening on board the liner "Ceramic" en route to New Zealand. Not alone did he astound the team colleagues who said it could not be done, but he also won the bet!

Played	Won	Drew	Lost	For	Against
29	22	1	6	570	174

Nelson/Marlborough/Golden Bay & Motueka	W 24-3
Buller	W 24-9
West Coast	W 32-3
Otago	L 9-23
Southland	L 0-11
NEW ZEALAND	D 9-9
South Canterbury	W 27-8
Canterbury	W 16-5
Ashburton County/North Otago	W 29-6
NEW ZEALAND	L 0-8
Wairarapa and Bush	W 27-3
Hawkes Bay	W 20-0
Poverty Bay/Bay of Plenty/East Coast	W 27-3
Wellington	W 12-6
NEW ZEALAND	L 3-6
Wanganui	W 21-3
Taranaki	W 25-3
Manawatu and Horowhenua	W 13-8
Waikato/Thames Valley/King Country	W 30-0
North Auckland	W 8-6
Auckland	W 32-9
NEW ZEALAND	L 8-11
New Zealand Maoris	W 14-9
New South Wales (Country)	W 47-3
New South Wales	W 22-6
AUSTRALIA	W 19-6
AUSTRALIA	W 24-3
Metropolitan Union	W 26-17
New South Wales XV	L 12-17
Ceylon (Unofficial)	W 44-6

Who was it coined the phrase that the All Blacks were "lucky to get nil" when beaten 12-0 by Munster at Thomond Park on October 31, 1978? Well whoever used it on that occasion, was actually stealing a line from Tom Reid, the Garryowen and Irish forward.

Tony O'Reilly, who toured with Reid on the 1955 Lions tour to South Africa, tells the story:

> Having seen Tom in action on tour when he was the 'cement' of the side, the 'mortar' that pulled us all together, I had not realised he was not noted for the avidity with which he trained. I'd last seen him in Pretoria as we boarded the plane to fly home and the following February we met again in London for the match against England.
>
> I noted in the dressing room that Tom was extremely vigorous in the pre-match warm-up and I said, 'for God's sake you'll exhaust yourself.' His reply was, 'Jesus, Reilly, this is the first run I've had since Pretoria.' He went out and, like all of us, proceeded to prove it was the first run since Pretoria, for we were hammered 20-0. Coming off the pitch pursued by every hospital orderly, fly-over constructor and trench-digger in the greater London area, I said to him, 'Wasn't that awful?' Back came the reply: 'Yes, Reilly, and weren't we lucky to get nil?'

O'Reilly has a very definite affection for Reid, respecting him far more than most of his colleagues on that tour and his subsequent tour to New Zealand in 1959. He comments:

> I should think the 1955 tour was the first time in his life that Reid was really fully fit and he played a major role in the success of the tour. We had won one and lost another of the first two tests and then we went 2-1 up in the series with a 9-6 win in the third

game. In my opinion, Tom Reid effectively won that game for us because of his dominance at the back of the lineout. He proved more than once that he was something other than a quick tongue and a golden voice and was one of the major successes of the tour, doing superbly in the two tests in which he played.

Reid was one of five Irish players on that side which drew the series 2-2 with South Africa. A quick-witted fellow, he had sharp competition in that field from Cecil Pedlow, undoubtedly one of the most accomplished athletes ever to wear the Irish jersey. Pedlow was a Davis cup standard tennis player, a squash international and a superb footballer who could kick with either foot. On tour, Pedlow was a regular try-scorer and goalkicker and ended up as top scorer with 58 points.

O'Reilly describes him:

In his own view, I think he lacked top pace for the wing but he was an outstandingly good utility player and deservedly got in for two tests. Off the field, he had a lightning Northern wit, captured by a story of a friend of mine who recently came to stay with us. He was writing a book about Belfast and when I told Cecil about this and introduced them, he replied: 'he'd better be quick!'

Pedlow had a great sense of fun. He had problems with his eyesight and he used to take off his glasses, always protesting to the girls that they should get closer to him so he could see them properly. But of course his eyesight also posed problems, especially under the high kick when he used to shout 'my ball' as it dropped 40 yards away! He was the perfect tourist and a man who could live with both victory or defeat at either personal or team level.

The 1955 side was captained by Robin Thompson of

Instonians, but unfortunately illness curtailed his contribution to the tour. He did play in three of the tests, but in the final game, when he came back after an operation for the removal of his appendix, he was not the same force he had been before his illness.

Robin Roe was capped 21 times for Ireland between 1952 and 1957 and the Lansdowne hooker gave sterling service to his country during that time, easily earning his place on the 1955 Lions tour. Unfortunately he came up against daunting competition from Bryn Meredith, described by O'Reilly as one of the greatest hookers he had ever seen in action. Roe had unfortunately damaged his ribs very early on in the tour and that kept him out of action for some time. Yet he played very well once he had recovered and was to become one of the most popular members of the party. Roe, who was a Protestant clergyman, came in for some ribbing because of the enormity of his 19-inch neck. The Catholics in the group used to tell him he had a great neck for a Roman collar. The Lansdowne man was noted for his achievements in areas other than rugby, winning the Military Cross in Aden while serving as chaplain to the British forces. "That did not surprise me. Robin Roe is a man with a strong sense of the heroic . . . a great man in many respects," says O'Reilly.

Fuzzy Anderson of Queen's University and NIFC was, according to O'Reilly, a world class prop-forward. He had played 13 times for Ireland by the time he was selected for the Lions. Unfortunately illness struck and he had to withdraw from the tour. O'Reilly remembers the Welsh game earlier that year: "I'll swear that Fuzzy was having a heart attack in the bath after that game. I looked at him and said, 'you look terrible.' Some time later he went into hospital for a full check-up and he had to undergo major heart surgery which obviously ended his rugby career prematurely."

All of these men, apart, of course, from Anderson, made a major contribution to that 1955 tour, and none did better than O'Reilly himself, who scored 16 tries, an achievement which made him the clear leader in that respect.

O'Reilly goes back over the story of his rapid rise to international rugby for Ireland and then selection on the Lions:

I had the good fortune of getting into the Irish team when I was only eighteen and a half. I played only three senior club games before being named in the Leinster team to meet Ulster, but I decided not to play — discretion being the better part of valour, since the conditions were very bad. I went climbing the Sugar Loaf instead and I learned a great deal about Irish rugby by not doing so. A reporter at the match decided the centres had not done too well that day and proclaimed that by comparison I must be the best centre in the country. By not playing, I did my prospects no harm and after one more club game, was named in the final trial, with my sixth senior game coming in an international against France.

The young Old Belvedere player did very well in his first season, well enough to be included in the 1955 Lions party which he was to serve so well. He enjoyed that tour thoroughly, although he said that when scoring his 16th try in the last minute of the final test, he dislocated his right shoulder and confesses that this was a weak point thereafter: "From the try-scoring point of view, I had a great tour, but I paid the price for it, for my shoulder problem was a recurring event and it troubled me greatly at times."

He singles out the Lions' backline as being almost completely responsible for his try-scoring spree:

I was at the end of a legendary backline, Jeeps, Morgan, Butterfield and Davies. What a way for the ball to get out to you! By the time the opposition had matched the threat of any one of that four, you were one on one. Right throughout my international career I had to face more than one defender, and once I became well known, I don't think I ever went

63

on the pitch without two or three guys determined to make a name for themselves by knocking me into the stand. In South Africa I was unknown, and that, for the first part of the tour at least, was a great advantage. With men like that inside me I got great scoring opportunities and got ten tries in my first six games. Things got a little tougher after that; I only scored six in my last ten matches and I suppose the aphorisms, which Cliff Morgan used to use are true: 'The gaps get smaller when your name gets bigger' and 'To be as good as you were, you have to be twice as good as you were.'

O'Reilly went to great pains to highlight the witty side of such players as Reid and Pedlow, but his own sense of fun is well documented. Even as a youthful 19-year old, he had begun to make his mark off the field. The manager of that tour was Jack Siggins of Collegians. O'Reilly says:

Jack was an excellent manager but he took himself a bit seriously early on ... that is, until Pedlow and myself got working on him, using sketches to press home our points. Thankfully he had the good humour to realise what we were at and as the tour progressed he became much more flexible and was very much one of the boys.

Played	Won	Drew	Lost	For	Against
25	19	1	5	457	283

Western Transvaal	L 6-9
Griqualand West	W 24-14
Northern Universities	W 32-6
Orange Free State	W 31-3
South-West Africa	W 9-0
Western Province	W 11-3
South Western Districts	W 22-3
Eastern Province	L 0-20
North-Eastern Districts	W 34-6
Transvaal	W 36-13
Rhodesia	W 27-14
Rhodesia	W 16-12
SOUTH AFRICA	W 23-22
Central Universities	W 21-14
Boland	W 11-0
Western Province Universities	W 20-17
SOUTH AFRICA	L 9-25
Eastern Transvaal	D 17-17
Northern Transvaal	W 14-11
SOUTH AFRICA	W 9-6
Natal	W 11-8
Junior Springboks	W 15-12
Border	L 12-14
SOUTH AFRICA	L 8-22
East African XV	W 39-12

If motivation was needed during the next Lions tour, then Irishman Dave Hewitt was surely the one to provide it. Sweat dripping from his brows in the fourth test against New Zealand in 1959, Tony O'Reilly wondered whether the Lions could hold out, even though they had scored three tries to two penalties by the All Blacks. He describes the action of that game:

> We had been beaten late in the first and second tests, had lost the third comprehensively but led 9-6 going into the final few minutes of the last. We were well on top but strange refereeing decisions had conspired to give them penalty chances. As they attacked, I stood on the goal line, deep in thought and thinking what my opposite number would do if he got the ball.
>
> Suddenly Dave Hewitt moved out towards me and with the crowd going crazy for an All Black score, says in a Northern Ireland accent: 'Have you seen that cloud formation up there. Why that's a very interesting and beautiful sky. I'm going to take a picture of that when this game is over.' I said to myself, 'My God, here is a man who is committed passionately to the game of rugby football!'

Hewitt was, by all accounts, a straight-forward man. He was the recipient of many presentations, being, as he was, one of the most popular players on tour. A typical reception might go like this — one of the rugby alickadoos would stand up and say: "We are pleased to have the Lions with us this evening, and particularly Dave Hewitt, because he is such a great player. We would like you, Dave, to have these six pieces of glass which we hope you will bring back to Ireland with you." Hewitt's stock reply was to say: "That's very kind of you; I am very pleased and thank you very much. But six pieces would be no good. I'd really need more than that." It was a joke, of course, but Andy

Mulligan, who joined the tour as a substitute, maintained that when the party left New Zealand, a 10,000 ton freighter followed carrying all the "loot" Dave Hewitt had been presented with on tour.

As well as the droll side of Hewitt, there was, of course, a very talented footballing brain. His international career began in 1958 and effectively concluded in 1962, although he did make a comeback in 1965. His biggest problem was injury, as he was prone to hamstring damage. But in the good times he was absolutely brilliant. O'Reilly recalls: "When Dave Hewitt was on his game, he was an unstoppable force. He was not always consistent, but for sheer brilliance he must rank as one of the best centres of all time. On that 1959 tour, myself, Niall Brophy and J. R. C. Young could, along with Dave, all do the 100 yards in less than 10 seconds. But Hewitt would leave us all for dead over 50 yards. Hewitt may only have come fourth in terms of try-scoring on that tour, but he was top scorer, for in addition to grabbing 13 tries, he kicked 20 conversions, 10 penalties and dropped a goal to give himself a total of 112 points."

Hewitt was one of ten Irishmen involved in that tour, although in the case of two of them — Niall Brophy and Mick English — the contribution was small. Brophy, who won 20 caps between 1957 and 1967, damaged an ankle without ever touching the ball. It happened, in fact, just before the kick-off in his first match of the tour and he never recovered from the injury. English, one of the greatest tactical kickers of a ball in the post-war era, was plagued by stomach strain and played only a limited number of games. He became known as "jog only". Manager Alf Wilson used to ask him before training whether he would be able to participate and when his condition was most acute, English would reply: "Sorry Alf, jog only." The two players finally returned home when it became clear that they would be unable to continue.

The 1959 side was captained by yet another Irishman, Ronnie Dawson, who, like Ciaran Fitzgerald 24 years later, was to go through some soul-searching as to whether he should select himself for the final test side. Again Bryn Meredith was in the party and posed an obvious threat. But when Dawson approached some of the players to ask their opinion, he was told that unless there was a very clear playing difference between himself and Meredith, he owed it to all of the players to keep himself in. He did, and they won that last match.

Dawson formed an all-Irish front for partnership with the redoubtable Sid Millar and Gordon Wood, two players of contrasting styles. Millar has been described as "a fattish centre three-quarter playing in the front row because of his ability to run, dummy sidestep, and pass without any difficulties whatever." Wood was less spectacular, but solid to the core, very fit and very strong — pretty immovable, in fact — and both made quite an impression when they played together.

In the second row was Bill Mulcahy who despite his lack of height, was one of Ireland's most successful forwards, winning himself 35 caps. He was arguably too small to be a second row, but yet had a high rate of success as a player. Cecil Pedlow, when asked by Tony O'Reilly what the line-out calls were before one international, replied: "Ah, just throw to the hole in the middle. They are crouching in a private trench." And Mulcahy himself, when asked how he would like the ball, is said to have reacted by saying, "low and crooked".

Mulcahy also suffered his share of injuries in New Zealand, but he was, according to O'Reilly, "never less than good and sometimes was superb. He was one of the most courageous footballers I have ever played with." The Bective Rangers man played in one test against Australia and one against New Zealand.

In 1955 the youngest member of the party was Tony O'Reilly. That distinction fell to another Irishman four years later. He was Corkman Noel Murphy, who was later to devote himself to coaching and managerial tasks as well. Ronnie Dawson described him then as a player whose basic talent was considerable. "He was the one above any of the others seen to be under the high dropping ball, showing no fear whatever." O'Reilly, in one of his many quick-silver comments, said of him: "All he wants to do is die for Ireland."

O'Reilly continued:

> Noel Murphy decided he'd make his name by standing under the high ball. I can still hear the New Zealand skies split by his high pitched cries — in a Cork accent of course — of 'my ball'. That only matched the shouts of 14 other guys shouting in unison 'your ball!'
>
> Murphy played extremely well. He was a damn good flank forward . . . not a player of blinding pace, nor was he a player of great broken field capabilities, but he had tremendous intelligence and had an instinct to be at the right place at the right time. He was not the flash type, but he was fearless and was always there to tidy up things.

Murphy's fine efforts won him a test place against Australia, and against New Zealand on three occasions during that long tour.

On every tour there are comedians, and if the 1955 duo of Pedlow and O'Reilly had split up, Andy Mulligan was there in 1959 to join the centre-turned-winger, O'Reilly — off the field, helping him amuse the team, as well as New Zealand rugby fans and radio listeners throughout the country, and on field setting him up for a then record-breaking number of tries by a touring player in New Zealand.

Mulligan, of Wanderers and London Irish, very nearly failed to make it. He was not an original selection, although tipped to be included in the party. When Scotsman Stan Coughtrie made the side before him, it came as a bitter disappointment to Mulligan for he had played extremely well in the international championship which had just concluded.

In any event, Coughtrie, a tall player for the position,

was injured and Mulligan was called upon as a replacement. O'Reilly takes up the story:

> The number one, Dickie Jeeps, had fathomless strength and absolute courage, but he was not a great runner with the ball. He had no break, was an adequate kicker and a short passer. With an out-half like Cliff Morgan, that would have been permissible, but with Bev Risman, in many ways as talented as Morgan but without the same speed, one needed a longer pass. Mulligan could out-pass Jeeps by a substantial margin.
>
> The big question was, however, whether Mulligan would stand up to the hard stuff with the All Blacks forwards coming through on him. He proved he was durable. Jeeps played in the first three tests but Andy, in fair competition, won his place for the last game, and I would say that the single most important determinant in making victory in that game possible was his play. It was his brilliant open side break, and a superb flying, diving reverse pass to Risman going down the blind side, with me having run into the centre to decoy the back row which led to the final try; and, of course, he also set me up for my 17th try to break Ken Jones's record. He broke quickly down the blind, drew my wing and left me with a 10-yard drive to the line.
>
> Mulligan's courage was beyond doubt even before that and after that game his jersey had to be cut off him, such was the extent of the injuries on his chest, ribs and stomach. He was bleeding quite heavily and his ribs were red raw for two weeks afterwards . . . but he helped win the game for us.

Off the field, O'Reilly, the contributor of 22 tries on a tour which embraced Canada in addition to Australia and New Zealand, was the perfect partner to Mulligan. Between them, they entertained the masses with their "goon show", easing the pressure when things got hot for the team and after several appearances on radio, actually took to the stage in the last week of the tour.

· Having already cut a disc, Mulligan and O'Reilly felt they had had enough training, yet they still had to participate. O'Reilly says:

> We needed some escape, so we signed on as a duet comedy team at the 'Hi Diddle Griddle' in Auckland, where I played the piano and Andy played the guitar. All went well because nobody knew we were there, but on the morning of the final test, there was this photograph which appeared in the local papers. Management were appalled. They had thought we had been in bed every night at 9 o'clock with our Horlicks!

An example of Mulligan's wit? Going for his first job he was asked as a final question: "What religion are you, by the way?" "Well sir, what religion had you in mind?" he quipped. Yes, those obviously were the days.

Played	Won	Drew	Lost	For	Against
33	27	0	6	842	353

Victoria	W 53-18
New South Wales	L 14-18
Queensland	W 39-11
AUSTRALIA	W 17-6
New South Wales Country Districts	W 27-14
AUSTRALIA	W 24-3
Hawkes Bay	W 52-12
East Coast and Poverty Bay	W 23-14
Auckland	W 15-10
New Zealand Universities	W 25-13
Otago	L 8-26
South Canterbury/North Otago/ Mid Canterbury	W 21-11
Southland	W 11-6
NEW ZEALAND	L 17-18
West Coast — Buller	W 58-3
Canterbury	L 14-20
Marlborough/Nelson/Golden Bay/ Motueka	W 64-5
Wellington	W 21-6
Wanganui	W 9-6
Taranaki	W 15-3
Manawatu & Horowhenua	W 26-6
NEW ZEALAND	L 8-11
King Country and Counties	W 25-5
Waikato	W 14-0
Wairarapa and Bush	W 37-11
NEW ZEALAND	L 8-22
New Zealand Juniors	W 29-9
New Zealand Maoris	W 12-6
Thames Valley and Bay of Plenty	W 26-24
North Auckland	W 35-13
NEW ZEALAND	W 9-6
British Columbia	W 16-11
Eastern Canada	W 70-6

CHAPTER 6

THE SIXTIES

Four of the seven Irishmen included in the tour party for South Africa in 1962 were already experienced Lions and two of the others were, later on in their career, to become household names in world rugby.

1962: SOUTH AFRICA

Arthur Smith's 1962 side may have lost the test series, but there was a fair element of bad luck involved, for having drawn the opening international, they lost the second game 3-0, and the third 8-3 — games which could have easily gone the other way.

Tom Kiernan, who with Englishman John Willcox was a full-back on the tour, recalls that the Lions should have won the second match. They had won a scrum near the Springboks' line and Bill Mulcahy, who was pack leader, called for a wheel. The pack drove over the home line and Keith Rowlands of Wales got the touchdown. The "try" however was not allowed by the South African referee, on the basis that he had been unsighted. Most Lions' sides have had problems with referees on overseas trips and the 1962 tour was no exception.

Kiernan quips: "Rumour had it that the try was disallowed because the referee did not know which of the Lions got the try!" South Africa had been leading 3-0 at the time and immediately after Rowland's claims for a score, the final whistle went, even though the visitors had been awarded a scrum five yards out.

Kiernan had not played in either the first or second internationals, a combination of ankle injuries and fine performances by Willcox damaging his progress, but he was included in the third test — one which the Lions might also have won. Included too that afternoon was Willie John McBride, who, like Kiernan, went on to become one of the best-known figures in the game. Both players will be dealt with in more detail later on in this book.

The former full-back and Irish coach had a great game that day, catching and kicking superbly and almost forging a try for Dickie Jeeps only seconds from the end. The Lions lost 3-8 but they might well have drawn, thus keeping the series on a "tightrope". With only a few minutes to go, they were level 3-3. In a desperate bid to win the match, they ran the ball from their own line and when a Richard Sharp pass went astray, Springboks' Keith Oxlee nipped in for the try which he converted himself.

It was a sad occasion for Kiernan and for three other Irish players — Willie John McBride, Sid Millar and Bill Mulcahy, who were in the side that day — but although the test series was lost, all of the Irish contingent earned praise for their performances throughout the trip.

McBride was the "baby" of the Lions pack at 21 years of age. He had only that season come onto the international team. He himself could hardly have expected to make the test side, but although excluded for the first two, he was named for the others. His selection came as a shock to some, to Keith Rowlands in particular, who made way for him in the third test.

But consultations with the record books and with those involved in the tour suggest clearly that McBride's rise to prominence was completely justified. He had shown steady improvement as the tour progressed, and in the 18th match against Transvaal — the last before the third test — his brilliant display of line-out jumping, rucking and capable scrummaging won him the test place. He returned the favour to the selectors by doing everything, and more, that was asked of him.

Haunted by an injury sustained three years before, Niall Brophy again had some problems in South Africa. Named in the side for the first test, he damaged a shoulder during the match, and although he played on, it clearly limited his participation for the remainder of the tour. He did come back to form to win a place against South Africa in the fourth match, but in all, he only played in five provincial matches, although he did score two fine tries. Brophy was to go on to win seven more caps for Ireland, two the following season, and then, after a period in the wilderness, five more in 1967, bringing his total to 20.

Bill Mulcahy was another player who had been to Australia, New Zealand and Canada in 1959, and this time around he was, with Sid Millar, the only Irishman to appear in all four tests.

Mulcahy won himself a large fan club in 1962. He led a big pack into battle with the Springboks and much of the credit for their success up front has been attributed to him. Long before the end of the tour, the pack were being referred to as Mulcahy's "Boyos". Mulcahy had, after his student days in UCD, moved on to Bohemians in Limerick, and he was the second player from that club to be honoured with selection for the Lions — the first being Mick English who had joined him three years before. But while he and Brophy (Blackrock) had left college, two more Irishmen were still involved in Universities rugby. Kiernan, of course, was still with UCC while Dave Hewitt, another veteran from 1959, was attending Queen's University.

It was not a happy tour for Hewitt, because like Kiernan he suffered greatly from injuries. He played in seven matches, whereas, if fit, would surely have participated in many more. He did score two tries and played in the last test, but as far as his Irish International career was concerned, he was almost finished. His last appearance for Ireland came in 1965 against Wales, after two full seasons of International activity.

Ray Hunter of CIYMS failed to make the test teams,

but scored two tries in 11 matches. Used as a utility back, he won a fair amount of praise at the time for his performances, and he was looked upon as an excellent defender. Hunter won a total of 10 caps for his country.

Millar of Ballymena was to go on to become one of the greatest Irish forwards of all time. A superb prop-forward, he was also a shrewd tactician and he gave pack leader Mulcahy incredible support. He played 16 matches in all; only Mike Campbell Lamberton, Keith Rowlands and Mulcahy were to play more than him. He won 37 caps for Ireland, his career extending from 1958 to 1970, and after that rugby still played a major role in his life, for following three Lions tours as a player, he went on to coach the brilliant 1974 team in South Africa, while six years later he managed Billy Beaumont's Lions.

Played	Won	Drew	Lost	For	Against
25	16	4	5	401	208

Rhodesia — W 38-9
Griqualand West — D 8-8
Western Transvaal — W 11-6
Southern Universities — W 14-11
Boland — W 25-8
South-West Africa — W 14-6
Northern Transvaal — L 6-14
SOUTH AFRICA — D 3-3
Natal — W 13-3
Eastern Province — W 21-6
Orange Free State — D 14-14
Junior Springboks — W 16-11
Combined Services — W 20-6
Western Province — W 21-13
South-Western Districts — W 11-3
SOUTH AFRICA — L 0-3
Northern Universities — D 6-6
Transvaal — W 24-3
SOUTH AFRICA — L 3-8
North-Eastern Districts — W 34-8
Border — W 5-0
Central Universities — W 14-6
Eastern Transvaal — L 16-19
SOUTH AFRICA — L 14-34
East Africa — W 50-0

Michael Cameron Gibson's international career began in 1964 and finished, 69 international appearances later, in 1979. With 12 caps for the British and Irish Lions, he is the most capped player in the world and that record is likely to remain for a long, long time to come.

By 1966, Gibson had won three Cambridge Blues and played for Ireland 13 times. But contrary to popular opinion, it was not "unlucky 13", for the Irish out-half, later centre, made a dramatic impact on Mike Campbell Lamberton's Lions party to the above mentioned countries.

This was a tour steeped in controversy. For a start, Campbell Lamberton was a surprise choice as captain, despite the fact that he had been a successful tourist to South Africa four years earlier. As it turned out, the big Scotsman stood down from some of the more important provincial matches and while he led the Lions to a series win in Australia and prompted them to their biggest ever win over that country in an International, Welshman Alun Pask, the vice-captain, would have been most people's choice for the captaincy.

However, despite Campbell Lamberton's leadership, it was obvious that Mike Gibson, one of eight Irishmen in the party, was the star of the show. In real terms, while Campbell Lamberton's Lions became the first overseas party to lose all matches in a series in New Zealand, they did not return with the worst record from that country, even if they came close to it. That distinction had fallen to the 1904 Lions who played five matches in New Zealand, winning two, losing two and drawing one. The 1966 team had a percentage of 60 wins, still better than the 1904 record and that of 1908, when an Anglo-Welsh side had an average of 55.8 per cent.

But back to the Irish link . . . and to Gibson, who was treated as star of the side wherever he went. Welshman David Watkins was the senior fly-half, playing in that position in all of the tests, both in Australia and New Zealand, but Gibson had blazed such a trail in provincial games that he just had to be included eventually. And he was: in the centre for the first test against the All Blacks, his partner being D. K. Jones of Cardiff and Wales.

Englishman Colin McFadyean, often the scourge of Ireland, was moved from the wing to centre and he partnered Gibson for the remaining three tests. Both men performed with distinction, even if they failed to stop New Zealand from battling on to the first ever series "whitewash".

Gibson was one of nine Irishmen in the party. Only eight were originally selected, but Barry Bresnihan of UCD was flown in as a replacement. Although he was confined to appearances in provincial games, Bresnihan, 25 times capped for Ireland, scored five fine tries.

As a youngster, Jerry Walsh was tipped for the top. Those who thought him good enough to make the grade at international level were right. From his early days at Presentation Brothers' College, Cork, he had starred in numerous schools sides. He won virtually every honour in the game including 21 caps for Ireland, until the final accolade, that of Lions selection, came to him. Hopes were high that he would figure in the selectors' plans for the test games. Sadly that dream did not materialise and he failed to make it, although he was a regular and fairly successful addition to the party. He scored three tries on tour.

The fourth Irish back on the tour was Roger Young, the Queen's University scrum-half, who had won nine caps at the time of the tour party announcement. Young eventually played for his country 26 times, before emigrating to South Africa. Young started out as number one scrum-half, but after two test appearances in Australia and one in New Zealand he lost his place. So from his point of view, despite some great performances, the tour ended in disappointment.

Ronnie Lamont failed to make the test sides in Australia, but a series of brilliant performances in New Zealand won him a place on the side and he never lost it after that. Lamont had a chequered career with Ireland, winning

79

seven caps in 1965 and 1966, and then losing his place, but returning for the entire 1970 season. In New Zealand he proved himself a worthy recipient of greater honours.

Noel Murphy had, as a youngster, been on the 1959 tour to the same three countries. This time he was older and wiser, but still only managed to play in the same number of tests as he had seven years before. There was a difference, for having played once against Australia and three times against the All Blacks on the previous tour, this time it was two and two, one of the games in the second row. He joined Barry Bresnihan, Mike Gibson, Ken Kennedy, Ray McLoughlin and Willie John McBride for the final international against Canada on the way home — a match which the Lions won by 19 points to eight and one in which Murphy scored two magnificent tries. He also scored in each of the Australian tests and had an overall total of six tries.

Willie John McBride was on his second tour, but his first trip to Australia and New Zealand, and as on the 1962 South Africa tour, he was a marvellous success. Like Lamont and Murphy, he had been one of the outstanding loose forwards, looking for work all of the time. No wonder then that he was to become such a great personality in the game in later years. His attitude was that everyone should give 100 per cent all of the time and there were many at the time who tipped him for greater honours.

Ken Kennedy was Ireland's most capped hooker, and he stands in the record books as such. Kennedy played two tests in both Australia and New Zealand and proved himself extremely popular both on and off the pitch. With Queen's, CIYMS, and later with London Irish, Kennedy won a total of 45 Irish caps and he was selected to travel with McBride's all-conquering 1974 side to South Africa.

Ray McLoughlin, then of Gosforth, of Blackrock, Connacht and Ireland, was arguably one of the foremost tacticians in the early 1960s. He was included in the 1966 Lions party and enjoyed considerable success. He appeared in the two internationals in Australia and one in New

Zealand, winning his place against stern opposition. He also returned to play in the international against Canada. McLoughlin lined out 40 times for Ireland, winning his first cap in 1962 and his last in 1975. In between he had a remarkable career and he is remembered as one of the best-known personalities of the game.

The manager of the party was also an Irishman. Des O'Brien was extremely well liked by the public and the media but unfortunately suffered because of a string of bad results. While accepted as a genuine effort-seeker, the general consensus of opinion was that he did not instil enough discipline in the players when necessary.

Played	Won	Drew	Lost	For	Against
35	23	3	9	524	345

Western Australia	W 60-3
South Australia	W 38-11
Victoria	W 24-14
Combined Country XV	W 6-3
New South Wales	D 6-6
AUSTRALIA	W 11-8
Queensland	W 26-3
AUSTRALIA	W 31-0
Southland	L 8-14
South Canterbury/North Otago/ Mid Canterbury	W 20-12
Otago	L 9-17
New Zealand Universities	W 24-11
Wellington	L 6-20
Nelson/Marlborough/Golden Bay/ Motueka	W 22-14
Taranaki	W 12-9
Bay of Plenty	D 6-6
North Auckland	W 6-3
NEW ZEALAND	L 3-20
West Coast/Buller	W 25-6
Canterbury	W 8-6
Manawatu/Horowhenua	W 17-8
Auckland	W 12-6
Wairarapa Bush	W 9-6
NEW ZEALAND	L 12-16
Wanganui/Kings Country	L 6-12
New Zealand Maoris	W 16-14
Poverty Bay/East Coast	W 9-6
Hawkes Bay	D 11-11
NEW ZEALAND	L 6-19

Played	Won	Drew	Lost	For	Against
35	23	3	9	524	345

New Zealand Juniors	W 9-3
Waikato	W 20-9
Thames Valley/Counties	W 13-9
NEW ZEALAND	L 11-24
British Columbia	L 3-8
CANADA	W 19-8

In every British and Irish Lion there is a determination to do well in the test series. After all, that is what the tour is really about. This was the case way back in 1888; it was the case 80 years later when Irishman Tom Kiernan became the sixth man from his country to lead the Lions.

Kiernan's job was a daunting one, for some of the players had been on Mike Campbell Lamberton's team two years before, and while it may be unjust to describe that as a disaster, it would be true to say that team spirit was not exactly at an all-time high. Kiernan's job, then, was not alone to ensure better results, but also to ensure that this tour would be a happy one, and that morale would be maintained throughout.

As far as results were concerned, he succeeded to a point. South Africa won the series 3-0, with one game drawn, and from that viewpoint the 1968 Lions failed in their mission. They managed, however, to return to these shores having won 15 of their 16 provincial matches and could, with a little luck, have done better in the tests.

Off the pitch, these tourists were the happiest bunch one could have met, even though some of their high-spirited moments prompted criticism in South African newspapers. There was talk of late night drinking parties and general misbehaviour. Most of the stories were quite untrue and were grossly exaggerated.

In his tour book, *On Trek Again,* Welsh journalist J. B. G. (Bryn) Thomas categorically denied that they were a "wild bunch", and said that while they were high-spirited, no serious complaints had been made against them. Most of the "sensational" stories had been written by pressmen who were not, in fact, travelling with the party and who had got second- and third-hand information. He described the players as "amenable tourists who were never any trouble to anyone, on or off the field".

Kiernan, manager David Brooks and coach Ronnie Dawson succeeded admirably in their aim — that of blending together players from four different countries. The 1966 tour and its problems were quickly forgotten.

A story told by Irish wing-forward, Mick Doyle, one of eight Irishmen in the party, confirms the determination to achieve that blend: "Syd Millar received a telephone call one night from a former Lions' colleague who had settled in South Africa. He, Tommy Kiernan, Willie John McBride and Ronnie Dawson were to be invited to his house. Millar refused, saying, 'all of us or nobody'. And they did not go."

It was a pity, then, that with such spirit and determination in the side, they were unable to do better in the series. The third test proved crucial, for it was here that the Lions could have squared it, and forced the Springboks to wait until the last game for their win. South Africa had won the first match 25-20, when Kiernan kicked five penalties and converted Willie John McBride's try. The second was a draw — 6 points all — but while the Lions went down 11-6 in the third game, they had enough chances to have won the game. Instead they lost and the Springboks hammered home their advantage in the last match of the tour by winning handsomely on a 19-6 scoreline.

Disheartening certainly, but things may well have taken a turn for the better had not this side been struck with a series of injuries to key players like Barry John, Gerald Davies and Gareth Edwards. Later on, Ireland's Roger Young was also injured and that necessitated the call up of Scotland's Gordon Connell, who had played just once for his country at that stage. At any rate, their tour average of 15 wins and a draw from 20 games was not disastrous, and was decidedly better than the previous tour to South Africa in 1962.

Kiernan, who had not particularly enjoyed himself six years before, emerged as one of the greatest full-backs of all time. Everything he did smacked of a great player, and if at times he had been criticised at home for rather inconsistent goalkicking, his flair for scoring proved a considerable advantage in South Africa. He was the second highest scorer on the tour, with 84 points, beaten only by England's

Bob Hiller who scored 20 more.

The Irishman was a popular choice for the captaincy. Ireland had enjoyed an excellent season in the international championship and Kiernan had been earmarked from the very beginning. The one threat may have been Welshman John Dawes, who, after being dropped by his country, came back to captain the side against Ireland in Lansdowne Road. As it turned out Ireland won and Dawes had to wait until 1971 to become a Lion.

Kiernan very much regrets that the team were unable to do better, but concedes: "We had a good, but not a great team. South Africa were just too strong for us, although I felt we might have had more success if we had avoided all those injuries." The Corkman, who since his last Lions tour had moved on to join Constitution, cannot be blamed for the Lions' lack of success, and his personal contribution was certainly one of the highlights. On tours of this nature, the pressure on players is often overwhelming. A large crowd awaited the arrival of the Lions on 13 May. Kiernan, as captain, was immediately approached by pressmen who wondered if, in preparation for his role as leader on the tour, he had learned some Afrikaans. "Tell me, Tom", asked one reporter, "do you understand our language?" "Of course I do — provided it's spoken through Irish," was the quick reply. That comment put him at immediate ease with his hosts and set the scene for a fruitful and happy relationship with his players.

Barry Bresnihan of UCD was known throughout the tour as "Doctor", for he was a medical student. A superb tourist, who was well known for his off-the-field renderings of Irish ballads, Bresnihan played in three of the test matches and in all played 15 times. He also managed to get Mick Doyle, his fellow countryman, drunk for the first time!

The said Mick Doyle, of Blackrock, and a Kerryman to boot, was one of the most lively members of the party, both on and off the pitch. In civvies, he made his presence felt wherever he went and once even introduced himself to a school of performing dolphins in a marine park. Although a witty character, who likes to look back on the funny side of the tour, Doyle took his rugby very seriously. He had been capped 19 times before embarking on the trip and made a determined bid to secure a test place for himself.

He suffered, however, from a lack of weight and height at the back of a line-out, where he was pitted against much bigger men. He soon made up for these deficiencies and proved himself a most worthy member of the party, playing in eleven matches, including the first test, when he was vice-captain. He was dropped for the second international and just as he was clearly challenging again, injury struck and that put paid to his chances.

Doyle has vivid recollections of the senior member of the playing party, Ballymena's Syd Millar, whom he described as "the old hand — the father figure". Millar, he says, did an immense amount of work to help some of the younger players cope with a tour of such length. "His nickname was Yogi Bear: he ate honey with his honey, and he came in for a lot of stick because of that. He was one of the fun people, a player's player, who had an enormous influence."

Millar played in nine games and propped in two tests. That brought his total number of appearances for the Lions to 44 (nine tests). Having already won 27 caps for Ireland, he went on to play on ten more occasions — only three short of Ray McLoughlin's Irish record for a prop-forward.

Much was expected of Mike Gibson following his brilliant displays in New Zealand and Australia two years before. Sadly, he failed to "ignite" the Lions as he had done then. He had his moments, but an injury early on seemed to have blunted much of his enthusiasm and when he came on as a reserve for the injured Barry John during the first test, it was clear he was not fully fit. Later on in the tour, he produced some flashes of magic as only he could do, but as the trip progressed, Gibson's form seemed to regress — not dramatically, but enough to damage the Lions' prospects of winning the series. In all, he made 14 appearances, playing in all the tests.

Roger Young, on his second Lions tour, was chairman of the "scrum-halves union" in South Africa, claiming that he should be the boss because he was older than Welshman Gareth Edwards. The two players became great friends despite the obvious rivalry between them and so it was a pity to see both eventually injured and out of the running for test places.

It was Edwards who seemed to be winning the duel, getting in for the first two tests, but then he was stricken with a hamstring injury and Young stepped in for the third. But Young, who had a fine tour, and often took physical punishment without complaint, was to be denied his second outing against the South Africans as he injured himself a couple of weeks before the final game. Yet he had some considerable success and received acclaim for his performance against Eastern Transvaal, the match which was to be dubbed "The Battle Of Springs". He scored two tries in nine appearances.

This was Willie John McBride's third Lions tour . . . and he was not finished yet! McBride made his presence felt in South Africa in a big way and was both feared and respected by the best of the Springboks. The tour was a personal triumph for him, because it was the first one in which he had played in all the tests. In the latter stages of the trip, McBride was, however, in some trouble, for he tore his leg in the first test and the wound became poisoned. The injury troubled him subsequently, and to a certain extent hampered him, even though he was still an automatic choice for the test sides.

Ken Goodall (City of Derry) might well have been an original choice for the tour but he was unavailable because of examinations. However, when Barry John was injured, and it became apparent that he was unlikely to take any further part in the tour, the selectors decided to replace him. The fact that they had only one recognised number eight in the party prompted them, not to look for a back, but for a forward.

His ambition of becoming a Lion realised, Goodall did not last long. During his first game against Eastern Transvaal he broke a bone in his hand, which ruled him out of further activity.

The Irish connection with this tour intensified with the appointment as assistant manager of Ronnie Dawson, who had virtually carte blanche on the coaching side. It was a major breakthrough, for Dawson, captain of the 1959 Lions, was the first man in that position to be given such an opportunity.

Played	Won	Drew	Lost	For	Against
20	15	1	4	377	181

Western Transvaal	W 20-12
Western Provinces	W 10-6
South-Western District	W 24-6
Eastern Province	W 23-14
Natal	W 17-5
Rhodesia	W 32-6
SOUTH AFRICA	L 20-25
North-West Cape	W 25-5
South-West Africa	W 23-0
Transvaal	L 6-14
SOUTH AFRICA	D 6-6
Eastern Transvaal	W 37-9
Northern Transvaal	W 22-19
Griqualand West	W 11-3
Boland	W 14-0
SOUTH AFRICA	L 6-11
Border	W 26-6
Orange Free State	W 9-3
North-East Cape	W 40-12
SOUTH AFRICA	L 6-19

CHAPTER 7

VICTORY AT LAST

Carwyn James, who has been said to be symbolic of
the recent swing toward coaching in the British Isles,
proved himself a coach of rare perception, wit and
intelligence. John Dawes, surely one of the shrewdest
midfield distributors the game has known, kept a firm
grip on the exacting job of tour captain. With firmness
from management and captain, the team found the
depths of character exceeding those of most touring
sides. Nor should Ray McLoughlin's technical advice
on forward methods early in the tour be forgotten.

Thus the 1971 tour of New Zealand was summed up by
my British colleague, David Frost of *The Guardian,* after
the Lions had returned home in triumph, having inflicted
upon the All Blacks their first defeat by a touring side
since 1937 and having taken the laurels for the first time in
that particular part of the Southern hemisphere.

1971: NEW ZEALAND

McLoughlin, arguably one of the most perceptive front-row
forwards of all time, was, however, lost to the tour after
a vicious bruising battle against Canterbury, a game which
the Lions won 14-3. In terms of the loss of playing
personnel, the win proved very costly. McLoughlin's
departure, a short time after the first test, was described at
the time as one of the tragedies of the tour, for it had been

91

pinpointed very early on that his influence on the forwards, not just as a player, but as a thinker, had been phenomenal. The Lions won the series with two victories, a draw and a loss, but there was a general feeling that with McLoughlin present, they would have done even better; indeed, a suggestion was put forward to allow him to stay on as forward coach, but of course this did not materialise.

That particular game was one the Lions wanted to forget rather quickly, but how could they? For not only did it spell the end for the classy McLoughlin but it also denied them the services of the established Scottish prop Sandy Carmichael, with Gareth Edwards and then two more Irishmen, Mick Hipwell and Fergus Slattery also having to face treatment for injuries afterwards.

Terenure man Hipwell had a chequered career for Ireland, being first capped in 1962, and then, when it looked as if his international tally would rest at two caps, he was recalled in 1968 when he won two more caps, got three more in 1969 (twice as a reserve) and was an ever-present in 1971 — perfect timing to help him win a place with the Lions party. In the early part of the tour, Hipwell had been playing so well that he was tipped to get into the test side but the tragic injury sustained in the Canterbury game was to deny him that honour. He was, along with John Taylor of Wales, selected for the team to meet New Zealand in the first test, but unfortunately the knee injury kept him out. He remained on with the party in the hope that the injury would heal, but in the week preceding the second test, he finally had to admit defeat. His injury, diagnosed by three specialists as a torn cartilage in his left knee, ruled him out entirely and so his early potential was not realised. He was replaced by Scotland's loose forward, Roger Arneil.

Slattery had teeth blown out in that explosive game with Canterbury, but the injury did not stop him from becoming one of the most impressive Lions on the tour. His international career had only begun the season before but by then it was clear that he would be on the scene for a long time. At 21 years of age he made his name quickly in New Zealand, scampering around in the open, bustling his opponents into error and deservedly winning his place for the third test. Like Hipwell, however, there was a sad twist of fate, for he fell ill with tonsilitis and had to withdraw from the team, forced to wait until the triumphant Lions tour to South Africa for a test place.

Sean Lynch, the St Mary's prop forward who went to New Zealand with little hope of making the test team, was thrust into the role of number one because of the injuries sustained by McLoughlin and Carmichael. Lynch was described as "a robust soul who had learned the facts of life running a Dublin pub. Like Carmichael and McLoughlin, Lynch had earlier been involved in incidents. Rather imprudently he held a jersey in a Maori match and the result was a punch in the mouth and 14 stitches. Lynch was an unyielding scrummager but because of a lack of ability at the lineout there was talk of him being replaced by Mike Roberts for the tests".

That of course did not happen; it was never really on, for Lynch made the transition from "dirt trekker" to test player virtually overnight. While the other prop forward replacement, Ian McLauchlan, was making a name for himself by scoring a try in the first test and impressing in the loose, Lynch was getting down to the basic important work of a man in his position: out scrummaging the opposition — and he did so with devastating effect. That was just the start of Lynch's international career which, in addition to the four Lions tests, was to give him 17 caps, the last in 1974 against New Zealand.

The now legendary Mike Gibson, who went on the tour as an out-half, settled into the test side in a different position, such was the form of Barry John, a player more restricted in his ability to change positions. Gibson was, of course, an automatic choice in the backline and if the New Zealand fans sang the praises of John more than once, the general consensus was that Gibson was the man of the tour. "The Complete Footballer", ran a headline in a newspaper, above an article expounding the virtues of Gibson following the 47-9 thrashing of Wellington. "Gibson's acceleration and deadly chops of direction were one of the main reasons why Wellington was so devastated," said the reporter. Everywhere Gibson went, he was sought after. On the pitch he more often than not got away from his pursuers; off it, he won himself some admiration for the way in which he coped with the adulation. Willie John McBride comments: "I believe thoroughly in the team game. I don't know whether players should be singled out. What I would say is that the 1971 team had a lot of magnificent backs and Mike, in the middle of that, played class rugby." And needless to mention, Gibson was selected for all four tests.

Willie John McBride was given the task of leading the pack when Ray McLoughlin was forced out of the tour and it was a challenge to which he responded excellently. He had his difficulties and conceded then, and many years later, that the series win was in some ways a lucky one. If, three years later, the pack which he led as captain in South Africa were to totally dominate their opponents, the same was not true in New Zealand. McBride says: "We never dominated them. We stole the first test when we got a lucky try and kicked two penalties but spent 75 minutes of the game tackling. They thrashed us in the second game. We played well for 20 minutes of the third match, scored 13 points and held on while the fourth game was, as the scoreline suggests, a very even contest."

But if McBride felt the Lions had their share of luck, he had little or no sympathy for the All Blacks. As he led the team in a victory song, "We Shall Overcome", at the post-match celebrations following the 9-3 first test victory, McBride was probably the most thrilled player of them all. It was McBride's 10th test for the Lions since his début on the South African tour in 1962 and it was the first time he had been on a winning side. "I have waited so long, too long for this", he announced. A great player, who had given such dedicated service to his country and to the Lions, McBride finally found a moment of joy in a test win which was to set the tourists on the road to that series victory and lift them out of a wilderness against the All Blacks. The mighty were finally to get a dose of their own medicine.

1971: NEW ZEALAND

Played	Won	Drew	Lost	For	Against
24	22	1	1	555	204

Counties/Thames Valley	W 25-3
King Country/Wanganui	W 22-9
Waikato	W 35-14
New Zealand Maoris	W 23-12
Wellington	W 47-9
South/Mid-Canterbury/North Otago	W 25-6
West Coast/Buller	W 39-6
Canterbury	W 14-3
Marlborough/Nelson Bays	W 31-12
NEW ZEALAND	W 9-3
Southland	W 25-3
Taranaki	W 14-9
New Zealand Universities	W 27-6
NEW ZEALAND	L 12-22
Wairarapa-Bush	W 27-6
Hawkes Bay	W 25-6
Poverty Bay/East Coast	W 18-12
Auckland	W 19-12
NEW ZEALAND	W 13-3
Manawatu/Horowhenua	W 39-6
North Auckland	W 11-5
Bay of Plenty	W 20-14
NEW ZEALAND	D 14-14

In 1974, McBride was coming to the end of an illustrious playing career and so when he was honoured with the captaincy of the Lions, it probably delighted him more than anything which went before, more even than the success in New Zealand.

In almost every Lions tour in modern times there has been some sort of controversy — disagreement, at any rate — about the choice of captain. McBride's selection was no different, for there were those who said he was too old at 33 years of age. He was due to celebrate another birthday in South Africa and on his performances there, no signs of mental or physical decay were in evidence. Quite simply, McBride was not alone a superb leader, but a magnificent player, confounding the few critics he had and leading the Lions to a spectacular 3-0 test series win. The Ballymena man recalls: "I was well aware of what people were saying, but I'm a queer sort of animal and the bigger the challenge the better I like it."

But he conceded that the success of the tour, during which his team's only blemish was a draw in the final test (and McBride says, "We won that one too"), was not due to himself:

> The key to that great tour was that each and every player in the party was prepared to die for one another and I personally received absolute loyalty. That to me was tremendous because the party was not a young one. Many of the players were long established internationals, players at the peak of their careers. It gave me great satisfaction that, knowing I was under pressure, they gave everything to ensure that the critics received their answer.

If McBride and Millar helped plot the downfall of the South Africans for the first time this century, there were many more who contributed. One of the foremost of these,

Fergus Slattery, probably played better than at any time in his international career, which had begun in 1970 and is indeed still continuing by the looks of things. Slattery, a roving, open-side flanker, with a particular ability to force the opposition into errors — a pressure player — reached, according to McBride, "the peak of the mountain".

McBride continues: "I dislike singling out any player in particular, simply because everyone was good, but Slattery contributed more to the winning of the bigger provincial and test games than any other player. He was everywhere, was so quick off the mark and he forced more errors amongst South African teams than anyone else."

Slattery played in all four tests and scored six tries in a total of 12 appearances. That would have amounted to seven, had referee Max Baise been on the spot to see him score what seemed a perfectly legitimate try in the last minute of the fourth test. The decision cost the Lions a 4-0 series win.

While McBride and Slattery were the only two Irish forwards to partake in the test series, the Bangor centre, Dick Milliken, who had been capped 10 times for Ireland up to that time, was carving out quite a niche for himself in the centre of the field for the Lions. Milliken, quiet, but yet very determined, struck up an ideal partnership with Scotland's Ian McGeechan. The Northerner had been living in the shadow of Mike Gibson for his own country, but with Gibson destined not to join the tour until well after it had begun, Milliken seized his opportunity superbly. Defensively he was most reliable and he proved he could score tries also, running in for five. He made a total of 13 appearances and along with McGeechan provided plenty of problems for the South Africans. A tribute is that even when Gibson arrived in the tour as a replacement for Alan Old and played well, the man who would have been first choice had he travelled out at the beginning could not displace Milliken. Milliken won four more caps for Ireland before a broken leg disrupted his international career.

The non-test Irishmen with the party were Tom Grace

and Johnny Moloney, both of St Mary's, Stewart McKinney (Dungannon), Gibson and Ken Kennedy; but the fact that they did not participate in the test series does not mean they had no roles to play. For a start, a decade ago there was no such thing as a medical officer, but Kennedy, being a doctor, was called upon many times during the day and night to administer to the injured. On the field Kennedy distinguished himself, but not enough in 10 appearances to dislodge Bobby Windsor from the hooking spot. Kennedy, like most of the Irish before and after him, was a popular tourist, although some of the referees and linesmen with whom he liked holding conversations might not always have agreed with that.

McKinney's tour appearances were confined to eight, mainly because of injuries, but his penalty goal against Free State, during a game which the Lions won 11-9, proved of vital importance in helping the Lions maintain their unbeaten record. McKinney was reputed to be one of the nicest players in the party and McBride endorses this: "The simplest things in life are probably the most important and are the most noticed at times. I can always remember as captain, the reaction of players when we visited certain places and the one thing you could say about Stewart McKinney was that when leaving, he would be the first person to say thanks to his hosts."

McKinney had been capped 10 times for Ireland before his tour to South Africa, and he was to go on to win a further 14 before finally playing his last game in 1978 against England.

Mike Gibson was unavailable for the tour at the outset, but he had intimated to the selectors that he would be willing to replace any injured player towards the end of June if the need arose. And so when Alan Old was the victim of a late tackle in a match against Proteas, he was called for. At 31 years of age, he had already been on three Lions tours, but this time there was no displacing Milliken or McGeechan in the centre. He was confined, therefore, to seven provincial matches, but he played very well in these and scored two tries as well as kicking a conversion. And his Lions appearances were not over, for he also travelled with the party to New Zealand three years later and in fact did not retire from international rugby until 1979.

Johnny Moloney, one of two St Mary's men in the side, had a disastrous start to the tour, dislocating his shoulder in the first match against Western Transvaal. That was the initial problem. The second was Gareth Edwards and even a fit Moloney would have conceded that his chances of gaining a test place would have been remote anyway. That injury and hamstring trouble towards the end of the tour confined him to eight outings, yet, in the matches in which he played, he did well. He scored three fine tries and displayed his qualities as a fast breaking half, an aspect of his play which severely troubled the opposition.

Moloney was matched as one of the humorists of the party by his club colleague, Tom Grace, whose impact on the tour took some time to show. He failed to make the test team, yet when he struck form he became a prolific try-scorer and by the end had crossed the line 13 times in eleven appearances — one more than his arch-rival but friend, J. J. Williams, who commanded a test position right through the series. That was some compensation at least for failing to win a place in the international games.

The 1974 tour was yet another example of the Irish contribution to Lions rugby over the years. McBride and coach Syd Millar, both of whom had worked in close cooperation with each other for some time before on the home scene, moulded together an all-conquering side which McBride later described as something akin to a machine:

> It was like something you turned on and off. You switched it on the morning of a game and off afterwards, so that the players not alone won their matches but also enjoyed thoroughly their visit to South Africa. The players were just not going to be beaten and Syd, I believe, had a great deal to do with that.

We had both been to South Africa before and knew something about the strength of the game there. That was a bonus. Syd and I both believe that rugby is about doing the simple things well. If one succeeds in doing that at this level, all the other natural skills and abilities fall into place, and he had the knack of encouraging players to allow those skills come to the surface.

But while we worked well as a team, it must also be said that 1974 was a good time in the four countries as far as rugby playing strength was concerned. Looking at the team before we left, it seemed very promising and in hindsight we did not have injury problems. We played four tests with just 17 players so there were some things which ran well for us. We had a fine pack, which was able to dominate the Springboks and the backs; all of them with inherent skills took it from there.

I believe another thing which helped us in South Africa was that we were very much alone. I was under a certain amount of pressure, but so was the rest of the party because of the political situation. Nobody at home really wanted us to be there and so we knew if we wanted to survive it had to be through our own efforts. Syd did more than anyone to instil that determination in the players.

Played	Won	Drew	Lost	For	Against
22	21	1	0	729	207

Western Transvaal	W 59-13
South-West Africa	W 23-16
Boland	W 33-6
Eastern Province	W 28-14
South-West Districts	W 97-0
Western Province	W 17-8
Proteas	W 37-6
SOUTH AFRICA	W 12-3
Southern Universities	W 26-4
Transvaal	W 23-15
Rhodesia	W 42-6
SOUTH AFRICA	W 28-9
Quaggas	W 20-16
Orange Free State	W 11-9
Griqualand West	W 69-16
North Transvaal	W 16-12
African Leopards	W 56-10
SOUTH AFRICA	W 26-9
Border	W 26-6
Natal	W 34-6
Eastern Transvaal	W 33-10
SOUTH AFRICA	W 13-13

CHAPTER 8

DEFEAT – AGAIN

The strains of touring were bound to take their toll. The Lions, having gained series wins in New Zealand and South Africa in 1971 and 1974, travelled once again to meet the All Blacks in 1977, but they had to do so without a few players who might well have made a difference.

Welshman Graham Price was making his Lions début on that tour and in 1983, while making his third trip with the Lions, he made some pertinent remarks about the sacrifices which players had to make in order to tour. Price was critical of the Home Rugby Unions for the way in which members of a Lions tour group are treated. He referred to the daily allowance which the players receive and while agreeing that the nominal sum was "fair enough because the players were getting paid by their employers anyway", suggested that the Unions should relieve the various companies of the burden which they had to endure.

It would be much easier, Price said, for players of the highest calibre, the most wanted men, as it were, to go on Lions tours if they could approach employers and ask for unpaid leave, with the Rugby Unions footing the bill. It was because of their reluctance to do so that players such as Gareth Edwards, J. P R. Williams, Mervyn Davies and Fergus Slattery were unable to travel, claimed Price.

1977: NEW ZEALAND AND FIJI

The 1977 tour was not the happiest in many respects other

than results. The Lions lost the test series 1-3; the management team of Scotsman George Burrell and John Dawes of Wales had become lonely figures by the end of the trip; and dreadful weather tended to make players miserable. English hooker Peter Wheeler managed to keep his sanity, however, and in a letter home a few weeks before the conclusion of the tour, wittily wrote: "Good news, it has only rained twice this week, once for three days, once for four days." That comment just about summed up the general feeling about the meteorological situation.

Although the tour was dogged by bad weather, the Lions came close to winning the test series, losing the first test 12-16 after All Black Grant Batty had got an opportunist try, winning the second game, but losing the next two, the last by just one point. The 1977 Lions played 26 games, scored 607 points and conceded 320.

Yet, despite all the problems, there were lively moments and many of them concerned the Irishmen in the side. The original selection included just three from Ireland — Phil Orr, Willie Duggan and Mike Gibson — but Moss Keane, or "Rent-a-Storm" as he became known on the trip, joined the party prior to their departure, having replaced the injured Geoff Wheel. As always, Keane, the great contributor, both on and off the pitch, made his presence felt early on. To other nationalities, Moss may be difficult to understand. So too, evidently, was manager Burrell, and there are reports of hilarious conversations between the two men.

In one, frustration finally got the better of the Irishman and he turned to Burrell saying: "George, for God's sake, am I talking too fast, or are you listening too slow?"

Moss has always been a bit of a hellraiser, but in a good-humoured sort of way. He has never done any harm to anyone, but as for shirts . . . well that's another story I can testify to. He seems to have this burning desire to see buttons popping!

Speaking of burning, no hotels were set on fire or anything during the 1977 tour, but the Fire Brigade were alerted on several occasions. Moss felt they should be out there doing something and so he and others conveniently arranged for them to have work. Invariably, however, when they got to the destination of the fire, it had been a false alarm. The Kerryman won himself such a reputation for this type of prank that when a "Court" session — a regular occurrence on tours of this nature — was arranged, Moss was appointed judge, but instead of being garbed in a cloak, his colleagues presented him with a fireman's hat!

Graham Price recalls Keane's hatred of flying:

> I shared a flight with him in 1977 from Palmerston North to Blenheim and Moss was terrified. He sat there with his left hand gripped to the seat in front of him as we made our way down the runway, and then I saw something which I have never seen before, or since. He picked this bottle of whiskey out of his bag with one hand, opened it with one hand and drank from it. All the time his other hand was clutched to the seat.

There was, and is, a more serious side to Moss Keane, and although he failed to hold his test place in New Zealand, having played alongside Allan Martin in the first test, he still had a fairly successful tour. While only playing five times in nine weeks after that opening test, Keane maintained his sense of purpose, and, of course, his humour.

From the playing point of view, Willie Duggan was the most successful of the Irish, winning a place at number eight in all four tests, and if he neglected a scoring chance in the last minute of the fourth test, which would probably have won the match, his all-round performances on the tour cannot be faulted. He was one of the outstanding forwards of the side and was respected by opponents and admired by his own side.

Duggan's determination knew no bounds and he was able to soak up punishment without complaining. Graham Price recalls his playing against the New Zealand Maoris. "He was the only number eight in a position to play, even though he should have been rested, having received punishment in a previous match. His back was virtually raw and to protect himself he was almost encased in padding. He was like a man with a parachute on his back going onto the pitch. Yet he never made it through the game. Some guy discovered that he had no padding on his face and hit him.''

Duggan was not short on wit either. Like Keane, he did not particularly relish the thought of training. The team's hotel in Christchurch had an elevator which regularly broke down. As the team awaited a bus to take them training one morning, Duggan and a few others were missing. Then it was discovered that they were trapped in the lift. Somebody managed to prise open the door wide enough to speak to them and he shouted: "Hang on a few minutes, we're getting somebody to fix the lift". Back came a prompt reply from Duggan: "We're not going anywhere. Just send us down some beer and sandwiches."

Mike Gibson was, at 34 years of age, the oldest playing member of the party. The magical genius which he had produced for Ireland and for previous Lions teams were missing on this occasion, however, although he occasionally played inspiring rugby. He was out of form in the early stages, but just when it looked as though he was improving, he suffered a hamstring injury. These two factors contrived to keep him out of the test sides, but he can still boast that he was the only player in the party not to have been on a losing side. In all he played 11 games.

Some of the press party on the 1977 tour were of the opinion that Phil Orr, the long-serving Irish loose head prop, was treated shabbily. Orr played in the first test which the Lions rather unluckily lost and he was said to have had a fine game. Yet he lost his place to Fran Cotton and only played in four more games out of 16. His scrummaging was controlled and in the loose he had a fine tour. If he had been allowed more matches, he might well have reestablished himself as the loose head. Instead, he was destined to sit on the bench no less than 11 times after that opening test.

Played	Won	Drew	Lost	For	Against
26	21	0	5	607	320

Wairarapa-Bush	W 41-13
Hawkes Bay	W 13-11
Poverty Bay/East Coast	W 25-6
Taranaki	W 21-13
King Country/Wanganui	W 60-9
Manawatu/Horowhenui	W 18-12
Otago	W 12-7
Southland	W 20-12
New Zealand Universities	L 9-21
NEW ZEALAND	L 12-16
South Canterbury/Mid Canterbury/ North Otago	W 45-6
Canterbury	W 14-13
West Coast/Buller	W 45-0
Wellington	W 13-6
Marlborough/Nelson Bay	W 40-23
NEW ZEALAND	W 13-9
New Zealand Maoris	W 22-19
Waikato	W 18-13
New Zealand Juniors	W 19-9
Auckland	W 34-15
NEW ZEALAND	L 7-19
Counties/Thames Valley	W 35-10
North Auckland	W 18-7
Bay of Plenty	W 23-15
NEW ZEALAND	L 9-10
Fiji	L 21-25

The 1980 tour to South Africa will go down in history as the most injury-ridden tour of all time. If the Lions thought they had problems with the rain of New Zealand in 1977, it was nothing to the difficulties encountered on the hard pitches of South Africa, when after the tour had begun, eight replacement or additional players had to be called for.

The Lions battle plan was disrupted time and time again as the spate of injuries began and continued. It was at times like Emergency Ward Ten. Welshmen Elgin Rees (an eve-of-tour replacement for Andy Irvine), Gareth Williams and Ian Stephens, Englishmen Paul Dodge and Steve Smith, Irishmen Tony Ward, John Robbie and Phil Orr, plus Irvine himself, were all called for at various stages of the tour.

Five Irishmen were original selections: Rodney O'Donnell (St Mary's), Ollie Campbell (Old Belvedere), Colin Patterson (Instonians), John O'Driscoll (London Irish) and Colm Tucker (Shannon); but before the end of the tour the representation jumped to eight, with the arrival of Ward, Robbie and Orr. In addition, they were managed by an Irishman — Syd Millar — and coached by an Irishman — Noel Murphy — both former Lions themselves.

Despite all the trials of the 1980 Lions, it is generally acknowledged that theirs was a more successful tour than that of 1977, even if they lost the test series by the same margin.

Millar was appointed manager after he finally agreed to take on the job, having first turned it down. A veteran of four tours to South Africa, one with Ireland in 1961, two with the Lions in 1962 and 1968 as a player, one as coach with the all-conquering 1974 Lions side and another as coach to a Rest of the World party to celebrate the opening of the new Loftus Versfeld stadium in Pretoria, Millar was just about the most experienced man around for the job. Management brings with it a certain amount of respon-ibility which, if not tackled properly, serves to divorce the coach from the players. But those same players thought highly of Millar, a straight talker who did not pull any punches. Graham Price says of him: "If he had something to say to a player, he just came straight out and said it. It might not have been always complimentary, but that type of approach is fair enough. Players sometimes need to be protected and Millar was great at ensuring we had our privacy when we needed it. Apart from that, he was a good manager."

Millar and Murphy had played 17 times for the Lions between them, a total equal to that of Willie John McBride's. To some, the Millar-Murphy combination may have been strange, given the fact that Millar is a North of Ireland Protestant and Murphy a Catholic from the South. And no doubt there was some fun attached to the fact that the team was announced on 17 March and the last test was played on 12 July. Of course, their union was not strange at all, because in Ireland there are no political or religious barriers in rugby circles. Protestants and Catholics, North and South, have all been playing rugby under the one banner for over 100 years and it is unlikely that that will ever change.

Murphy is a tee-totaller, but has always been known to act drunk in a party mood. In the 1980 tour he was just as much involved in players' activities as he was in management's. According to Price, "he was just one of us". But while Murphy's drinks were non-alcoholic, it is a fact that once on tour he did get tipsy. While celebrating a victory one evening, Murphy was indulging in his favourite minerals, completely unaware of the fact that his drinks were being laced with vodka in increasing amounts as the night went on. The following morning he complained of a headache, but to this day he insists that the alleged mischief could not have happened. The players insist that it did.

The biggest surprise choice for the tour was surely Colm Tucker, the big Shannon flanker, who had played just twice for Ireland, once as a reserve. But Tucker had established himself long before the end of the tour and played a dynamic role in the last two tests, helping the Lions to a victory in the fourth — the first time South Africa had gone down in a final test to the Lions. The Lions lacked a flying wing-forward on that tour and Tucker seemed to be the only one to help them out, even though he was forced to play a role he may not have been suited to. In the circumstances he did tremendously well and was one of the big successes of the tour.

Maurice Colclough, the big English second row, spent a lot of time in the company of John O'Driscoll on the tour, but very rarely met his "friend". O'Driscoll is the quiet man of rugby, friendly and serious. But there is a fun side to him and that is why Colclough refers to him as "O'Driscoll and his friend". In South Africa, O'Driscoll was regarded as one of the most consistent members of the party, being rewarded with a place in each of the four tests and scoring a try in two of them — the only one to do so.

The tour was to end in tragedy for impish Irish scrum-half Colin Patterson who, after the injury to Welshman Terry Holmes, established himself as number one choice. In any event, Patterson received some rave reviews for his performances and he played in three tests, before he received a catastrophic knee injury in the last game prior to the final test. Patterson, the smallest and lightest player, had had to give up his job as a solicitor to make the tour, his firm having complained so much when he toured Australia the previous year that he decided there was no point in asking for leave for 10 weeks. It was to prove costly in more ways than one, for the injury, which was said at the time to be the most serious ever of that type, left his international career in ruins.

Ollie Campbell was to have his share of injury problems too and was ruled out of eight of the first nine matches because of hamstring trouble. But the golden touch was still there when he did play, and he scored in all but one of his appearances, the exception being in the second test when he came on as a replacement for Gareth Davies. Campbell was, predictably, the tour's top scorer with 60 points, and that was achieved despite the fact that he had been injured for so long. A great admirer of Campbell's on that tour was Clive Woodward, who accredited Campbell with some of his own scoring success. Woodward finished second to Campbell with a total of 53 points which included five conversions and eight penalties. The Englishman said at the time: "Campbell taught me that successful goalkicking was all about getting the run-up correct."

Reserve John Robbie was unique in that he was the only player to line out in a test who did not play on a losing side. He appeared on seven occasions and had an exceptionally good test. He scored seven points, which he achieved through a try and a drop goal in the second-last game of the tour, against Griqualand West.

Phil Orr had a quiet tour and while he played five games, he appeared only in one "Saturday" match. Although Tony Ward was destined to be dropped to the mid-week side and only got five games, he still won a test place and in the process made his mark in the history books by scoring a record 18 points in the first test.

The Irish, it has been said, time and time again, are colourful tourists, but in 1980, Rodney O'Donnell must surely have beaten the lot of them. O'Donnell was notoriously superstitious. He was a talking point before the group ever left London and was constantly the butt of pranks by his fellow players. On the rugby pitch, O'Donnell would always take care to step over, rather than on, straight lines, and if the opposition scored a penalty or a goal of another nature, he would always throw the ball back over the crossbar. Off the pitch, if he trod on a line, he would re-trace his steps. Getting into bed turned out to be a rare old ritual: all wall hangings had to be perfectly straight and the bed covers back. Then he would charge onto the bed, taking care not to touch the bed covers, and hitting the bottom sheet first. He always refused to take a room where the numbers added up to 13 and was horrified on Friday 13 June when his team mates decided to play a joke on him. When he left his room, they plastered the number 13 all over the door and they chalked straight lines all over the floor of the corridor. To make his exit impossible, they replaced the various numbers on the lift with the number 13. O'Donnell immediately retreated back to his room and told them they would have to carry him out. That, in the end, is what happened.

O'Donnell had won himself a place in the first test, and although dropped for the second, was still in contention for a place. However, an injury he received when playing against the Junior Springboks in the 12th match of the tour put paid to his aspirations. While tackling one of the opposition, he damaged his neck, and the injury was so serious that it forced him to retire early from the game.

Played	Won	Drew	Lost	For	Against
18	15	0	3	401	244

Eastern Province	W 28-16
South Africa Rugby Association Invitation team	W 28-6
Natal	W 21-15
South African Invitation XV	W 22-19
Orange Free State	W 21-17
Sarf Federation Invitation XV	W 15-6
SOUTH AFRICA	L 22-26
South Africa Country XV	W 27-7
Transvaal	W 32-12
Eastern Transvaal	W 21-15
SOUTH AFRICA	L 19-26
Junior Springboks	W 17-6
Northern Transvaal	W 16-9
SOUTH AFRICA	L 10-12
South African Barbarians	W 25-14
Western Province	W 37-6
Griqualand West	W 23-19
SOUTH AFRICA	W 17-13

CHAPTER 9

TRIPLE CROWNS AND THINGS

Irish rugby was at a low ebb as the 1981/82 international championship approached. A run of seven successive defeats, the last against Australia just a few months before, did not augur well for the matches to come.

The record books show that Ireland had been white-washed in the previous season's championship, that they lost twice to South Africa, that they were beaten by Australia and that, in fact, before this succession of defeats they could only draw 13-13 with Romania.

But had the Irish really performed so badly? They lost two of the championship matches by just one point, being beaten by Wales 9-8, despite having scored the only tries of the game. They ran fancied South Africa close on a tour where some of the top Irish players were not available.

WALES

After the match with the Wallabies and the Irish trials, five changes were made for the Lansdowne Road clash with Wales. Fergus Slattery had abdicated as captain, but remained on the side, and that role was given to Ciaran Fitzgerald who returned to replace John Cantrell. Fitzgerald was first capped by Ireland on the 1979 tour to Australia and he retained his place for the ensuing championship season, before losing his place. The decision to award him the captaincy was to prove of paramount importance in Ireland's dramatic comeback.

Ollie Campbell, whose inclusion in the Irish team for the test matches against Australia in 1979 shocked the rugby world, did not play in the Lansdowne Road game against the Aussies, but returned again for the new championship season, with Tony Ward being excluded. Corkman Moss Finn had sampled less than 40 minutes of international rugby in 1979, when he played against England, before having to retire with an injury. The former schools' star seemed destined to be a "one hit wonder". But now he was named instead of Terry Kennedy on the left-wing. Gerry McLoughlin of Shannon also won back his place from Mick Fitzpatrick, while Moss Keane was named instead of Brendan Foley. No disrespect to the men they replaced, but each and every change had a crucial bearing on Ireland's destiny over the next four games.

Ireland's spell in the wilderness was over . . .

"Ireland, Ireland, Ireland", chanted thousands of supporters as their heroes were carried shoulder-high to the dressing rooms, having defeated Wales 20 points to 12 in their first match at Lansdowne Road. Pride had been restored and Irish rugby was on the way back.

Wales, despite the scoreline, had been routed by an Irish pack which had worked feverishly to ensure that Fitzgerald's début as a captain would be a winning one. Slattery, John O'Driscoll and Willie Duggan were rampant. Keane, celebrating his 40th cap, was back in his best form alongside the Corkman Donal Lenihan of UCC, whose exhibition of line-out play was too much for Richard Moriarty and Geoff Wheel to contain. And in the front row, prompted by the display of Fitzgerald, Phil Orr and the recalled McLoughlin played their parts.

But if the forwards were a powerful force, the men behind them proved their resourcefulness in a manner which was not only pleasing to watch but also effective. They made a stunning contribution, although robbed of their two first choice centres, David Irwin and Paul Dean, both of whom received injuries before half-time. Ireland's reserve strength was decisive, for Irwin and Dean were replaced by two top class players in Michael Kiernan and John Murphy. From scrum-half Robbie McGrath out, the Irish backs held the edge, denying Wales clean breaks and thrusting forward in numbers themselves, with possession expertly won from the pack.

Wales went ahead within three minutes of kick-off when Gwyn Evans kicked a penalty goal, but 20 minutes later, Lansdowne Road erupted when right-wing Trevor Ringland got in for a try at the corner. A Campbell chip was followed up by Orr and Slattery. They won the ruck, McGrath went blindside and Irwin's perfectly timed pass allowed Ringland space; his strength in charging through a Gareth Davies tackle gave Ireland the try, and proved to be one of the main talking points of the game.

A typical Terry Holmes try followed and Evans kicked the conversion to give Wales a six-points lead, but just before the break, Campbell exposed the weakness in the Welsh back row with a beautiful blind side run and then a scoring pass to Finn in the left-hand corner.

After that, it was all Ireland. Fired by another brilliant try by Finn five minutes after the resumption, they tore into Wales. It was a barrage of continuous pressure. Campbell, who had converted Finn's second try, kicked a penalty to stretch the lead to 17-9 and while Gary Pearce, substitute for the injured Davies, dropped a goal for Wales, Ireland were in no danger. Further pressure paid off by way of a Campbell penalty before the finish.

ENGLAND

Ireland were on course for the Triple Crown, no doubt about that and if the record books show that they won by the narrowest possible margin, their 16-15 victory in the next game was every bit deserved.

England's try came only in the dying seconds of the game and it served only to put a flattering look on the scoreline. It came far too late to make any difference, because as Ollie Campbell prepared to re-start the match, referee Alan Hosie of Scotland signalled the end.

The English clearly missed captain Bill Beaumont, whose head injury sustained a couple of weeks earlier forced him into retirement, but Ireland cannot be denied a win achieved against the odds.

England did much of the pressing early in the game, but Ireland soon found their feet and once again the forwards are due a tremendous amount of praise for the win, with Lenihan and the rest again stamping their class on the contest.

Campbell put in another world class performance, taunting England with inch-perfect tactical kicking and some explosive running. He helped set up their vital second-half try and then converted it into the teeth of a gale — points which, in the end, were so important.

Kiernan was horribly unlucky not to have scored a try which would have been a classic, but he will be remembered for a kamikaze-style tackle on English full-back Marcus Rose midway through the second-half, while Hugo MacNeill, apart from scoring his third international try, was so solid at full-back that he made Huw Davies, the English out-half, look very ordinary indeed.

England had their moments, particularly in the first few minutes, but it was Ireland who took the lead with a penalty by Campbell. Twice they nearly scored tries, Kiernan being called back for a forward-pass infringement and Slattery denied his moment of glory when most felt he had scored. But from there, they finally got the score they deserved. Ireland had been awarded the scrum and MacNeill came into the line on the blind to take the pass from McGrath and get in near the corner. Rose made his effort to stop him much too late.

Rose kicked England's opening points from a penalty soon afterwards but when Mike Slemen was caught in possession by Ringland near his own line, England were penalised and Campbell kicked the resultant penalty to give the Irish a 10-3 half-time lead.

Rose kicked another penalty for England within minutes

of the re-start but although they threw everything into attack, a great defence and some mistakes by a rather inept-looking English backline combined to deny them success. Those factors, in addition to a concerted effort by the Irish pack and a break of real quality by Campbell which culminated in another Irish try, contrived to smash the English challenge.

The all-important score came after 14 minutes. Stand-in captain Steve Smith put the ball crookedly into a scrum near his own line and was penalised. Campbell attempted a drop at goal but Smith, amazingly, blocked it down. The ball, however, broke favourably for Ireland and Campbell ran to his right, linking up with his forwards. The move finished with McLoughlin sweeping over the line, the whole pack driving from behind. Campbell converted from the touchline.

Ireland controlled the game after that until England's late surge which brought them a try from left-winger Mike Slemen, one to which Rose added the points. A good one, but too late.

SCOTLAND

The attitude of Maurice Ignatius Keane — "Moss" for short — typified the approach by the Irish to their golden opportunity to seal the Triple Crown at the Lansdowne Road headquarters of the Irish Rugby Football Union, for the first time.

One of the senior members of the side, a player who might well have been lost to the game but for his academic distinctions at University College, Cork, the big Kerryman, a former Gaelic footballer, said: "This is the last chance for a lot of us. We are not over-confident. Every one of us knows how difficult Scotland are going to be. They are an excellent side and I can assure you that nobody knows this better than the Irish team. It would be foolish to think that the Triple Crown is ours."

Thus there was a cautious build-up to the final match of

Ireland's Triple Crown tests, held in Dublin on 22 February 1982. Ireland had failed at the last hurdle on more than one occasion, and while the public were euphoric and confident, the team were, more than anything else, determined.

As Ciaran Fitzgerald led Ireland onto the pitch, there was a glow in his eyes, but yet his face was etched with emotion. The roar went up, the game was on and Ireland were 80 minutes from glory.

Two minutes into the match, scoring supremo Ollie Campbell put Ireland ahead with a 40-yard penalty goal and after eight minutes he struck again with a second. But Irish hearts beat a little faster in 14 minutes when Roy Laidlaw and John Rutherford combined brilliantly for the out-half to fly past the Irish defence, scoring near the posts. Andy Irvine converted.

The Irish pack, after that lapse of concentration in the back row, were not, however, to be denied. They continued to impose themselves and as the Scottish eight began to wilt under tremendous pressure, the scoring chances came. Campbell kicked two penalties and dropped a goal, building up the half-time lead to one of nine points — and it could have been more, for he missed two kicks before the break.

But he got further chances and a penalty ten minutes into the second half damaged Scotland's chances considerably. Jim Renwick did kick a penalty 10 minutes later, having taken over the kicking duties from Irvine, who was sadly out of form, but Campbell got another with nine minutes remaining and a second penalty from Renwick was really only of cosmetic value.

Fans wept openly when the final whistle went and it took the players several minutes to make it to the safety of the dressing rooms where, inevitably, a case of champagne awaited them.

That celebration was only the start. Men like Keane, Fergus Slattery and Willie Duggan, the veterans of the side, had waited for a long time for it. So too had coach Tom Kiernan who had played 54 times for his country between

1960 and 1973, but had never been on a Triple Crown winning side.

Many stories will be told in the years to come, but one comment from Keane is particularly choice: "You know why Kiernan ensured us old boys were kept in — he wanted some link between his lot and the Triple Crown."

Later, as Keane left the traditional after-match "watering hole", O'Donoghue's upstairs lounge in Merrion Road, a tall woman approached him: "Oh My God, what a darling man." He, and fourteen others.

FRANCE

Le Crunch for Ireland came in Paris when hopes of a Grand Slam were lost. They were beaten by a better side on a day when little went right for them and when a number of factors conspired to act against them.

The five-week gap after the Triple Crown win may have played a part, for after that achievement it was probably difficult to approach the French game with the same enthusiasm, even if further honours were at stake.

The loss of number eight, Willie Duggan, on the eve of the game was also a crushing blow. His experience at the tail of the line-out and his no-nonsense approach was badly missed. John O'Driscoll was moved from wing-forward and Ronan Kearney of Wanderers came into the side. The two did their best, but neither O'Driscoll in his new role or Kearney were able to get the better of Frenchman Jean Luc Joinel who had a storming game.

It must be remembered too that the French side selected for the match was a very different one from the teams which had stuttered their way through the championship. The "heavies" were brought back, and that was to prove decisive. In the very first minute of the game, English referee Alan Welsby seemed to lose control of the French. Irish prop forward Gerry McLoughlin was penalised and warned for punching an opponent. Yet the referee did not see fit to speak to two Frenchmen who had kicked and punched McLoughlin whilst on the ground, a performance which had prompted his retaliatory action.

The punching, the gouging and the butting went on almost throughout. The intimidating atmosphere of the *Parc des Princes* had an inhibiting effect on the Irish, and seemingly on the referee too, for rarely did he take action against a side which was determined to win — one way or the other. The sad thing was that when France began to play rugby, they did it well; and most probably they would have won anyway, but their tactics left a bitter taste.

Ireland held a 6-3 half-time advantage with Campbell kicking two penalties after Serge Blanco had given France an early lead with a penalty. France, however, took the lead again with a Blanco try early in the second half and both he and Gabarnet (2) kicked penalties to put the issue beyond reach. Campbell did kick a penalty, but on the stroke of full-time, France broke through again and Patrick Mesny got in for a try which Gabarnet converted.

THE TEAMS

IRELAND v WALES

Ireland. H. MacNeill (Dublin University), M. Ringland (Queen's), D. Irwin (Queens), P. Dean (St Mary's), M. Finn (Constitution), O. Campbell (St Mary's), R. McGrath (Wanderers), P. Orr (Old Wesley), C. Fitzgerald (St Mary's; capt.), G. McLoughlin (Shannon), M. Keane (Lansdowne), D. Lenihan (UCC), F. Slattery (Blackrock), W. Duggan (Blackrock), J. O'Driscoll (London Irish). Reserves: M. Kiernan (Dolphin) for Irwin, J. Murphy (Greystones) for Dean.

Wales. G. Evans (Maesteg), P. R. Ackerman (Newport), P. Daniels (Cardiff), D. Richards (Swansea), C. Rees (London Welsh), G. Davies (Cardiff, capt.), T. Holmes (Cardiff), I. Stephens (Brigend), A. Phillips (Cardiff),

G. Price (Pontypool), R. Moriarty (Swansea), G. Wheel (Swansea), M. Davies (Swansea), J. Squire (Pontypool), G. Williams (Brigend).
Referee: J. Short (Scotland).

IRELAND v ENGLAND

England. M. Rose (Cambridge), J. Carleton (Orrell), C. Woodward (Leicester), T. Bond (Sale), M. Slemen (Liverpool), H. Davies (Cambridge), S. Smith (Sale; capt.), C. Smart (Newport), P. Wheeler (Leicester), P. Blakeway (Gloucester), J. Sydall (Waterloo), M. Colclough (Angouleme), N. Jeavons (Moseley), J. Scott (Cardiff), P. Winterbottom (Headingly).

Ireland. H. MacNeill (Dublin University), T. Ringland (Queen's), M. Kiernan (Dolphin), P. Dean (St Mary's), M. Finn (Constitution), O. Campbell (Old Belvedere), R.McGrath (Wanderers), P. Orr (Old Wesley), C. Fitzgerald (St Mary's, capt.), G. McLoughlin (Shannon), M. Keane (Lansdowne), D. Lenihan (UCC), F. Slattery (Blackrock), W. Duggan (Blackrock), J. O'Driscoll (London Irish).
Referee: A. Hosie (Scotland).

IRELAND v SCOTLAND

Ireland. H. MacNeill (Dublin University), M. Finn (Constitution), M. Kiernan (Dolphin), P. Dean (St Mary's), K. Crossan (Instonians), O. Campbell (Old Belvedere), R. McGrath (Wanderers), P. Orr (Old Wesley), C. Fitzgerald (St Mary's, capt.), G. McLoughlin (Shannon), M. Keane (Lansdowne), D. Lenihan (UCC), F. Slattery (Blackrock), W. Duggan (Blackrock), J. O'Driscoll (London Irish).

Scotland. A. Irvine (Heriots), K. Robertson (Melrose), J. Renwick (Hawick), D. Johnston (Watsonians), R. Baird (Kelso), J. Rutherford (Selkirk), R. Laidlaw (Jedforest), J. Aitken (Gala), C. Deans (Hawick), I. Milne (Selkirk),

B. Cuthbertson (Kilmarnock), A. Tomes (Hawick), J. Calder (Stewarts Melville), I. Paxton (Selkirk), E. P. Paxton (Kelso).
Referee: C. Norling (Wales).

IRELAND v FRANCE

France. S. Gabarnet (Toulouse), S. Blanco (Biarritz), P. Mesny (Grenoble), C. Belescain (Bayonne), M. Fabre (Beziers), J. P. Lescarboura (Dax), P. Berbiziers (Lourdes), R. Paparamborde (Pau), P. Dintrans (Tarbes), P. Dospital (Bayonne), J. F. Imbernon (Perpignan), D. Revallier (Garulhet), L. Rodriguez (Mont de Maisan), J. L. Joinel (Brive), J. P. Rives (Toulouse, capt.).

Ireland. H. MacNeill (Dublin University), T. Ringland (Queen's), M. Kiernan (Dolphin), P. Dean (St Mary's), M. Finn (Constitution), O. Campbell (Old Belvedere), R. McGrath (Wanderers), P. Orr (Old Wesley), C. Fitzgerald (St Mary's, capt.) G. McLoughlin (Shannon), M. Keane (Lansdowne), D. Lenihan (UCC), F. Slattery (Blackrock), J. O'Driscoll (London Irish), R. Kearney (Wanderers).
Referee: A. Welsby (England).

SCOTLAND

Small sections of the British media who took none too kindly to Ireland's Triple Crown began to write them off again before the start of the 1982/83 season. Not even the success of the previous year stopped Ireland from being termed "Dad's Army", an endearing title in some quarters, but in others, meant as less than complimentary.

And so as the new international season approached, England were being put forward as potential champions. Few suggested that Ireland could maintain their run. But Fitzgerald, the "old boys" and the younger members of the side were to prove critics wrong again. Certainly they failed against Wales; their performance that day was dismal,

122

as the Welshmen reached their full potential for the first, and last time in the championship. But as they say, three out of four ain't bad, and Ireland finished the season with three wins, six points and a share of the championship. Their 71 points total was the biggest ever by an Irish side and supreme goalkicker Ollie Campbell notched 52 points for himself — and that included his first try.

Jim Renwick, one of the most experienced of the Scottish players and also a Lion, predicted that the Irish might well win their sixth Triple Crown, after they had defeated his own country in Murrayfield in their first match of the season: "Ireland took their chances and fully deserved their victory. The character of the side was shown in the last quarter when we launched our assault."

It was, in fact, the tremendous commitment, dogged determination and quite brilliant defensive work in those last 20 minutes which swung the issue Ireland's way in a match which was always closely contested and which exploded into life in stages.

Scotland might well point out that the woodwork foiled them of a draw, but when the dust settled, few could argue that Ireland in every respect except the scoreline garnered a handsome victory, which was their first at Murrayfield since 1971.

It was stirring stuff, with Ireland hammering home a firm first-half advantage and then showing consistency and character as the expected second-half Scottish bombardment materialised. There were times when the Irish sagged, but under pressure they were to prove indestructible. Their efforts were highlighted by a remarkable display at full-back by Hugo MacNeill, who did nothing wrong all day, and his team-mates responded with superb covering and first time tackling when needed most.

The "Dad's Army" pack were on top for much of the game. They won the rucks and mauls and the lineouts, with Donal Lenihan in firm control out of touch.

Ollie Campbell may have been more subdued than normal but the Scottish back row — Jim Calder, Iain Paxton and David Leslie — were unable to keep him under "wraps" completely and that was crucial. Campbell made another big contribution on the scoreboard, with 11 points, and Michael Kiernan scored his first international try, one created for him by the try-scoring winger, Moss Finn.

Ireland were firmly in the driving seat at the half-time break. Campbell kicked a penalty in the 14th minute, and after a shock try by brilliant Scottish scrum-half Roy Laidlaw, they regained their composure. Campbell kicked his second penalty after 24 minutes and Ireland threw everything into attack with the rewards coming late in the second half. Five minutes from the break, Ireland worked a beautiful move with Moss Finn thundering in from the left-wing to take a pass in the centre of the field. He split the defence and when checked, chipped to his left where the speedy Kiernan had positioned himself. He won a neck-and-neck battle for possession against full-back Peter Dods to get the try which Campbell converted. And in injury time, the out-half grabbed the points which secured Ireland's win, when he kicked his third penalty.

Scotland charged back at them in the second half and Jim Renwick, with a drop goal and Dods, with two penalties, set the scene for a grandstand finish. But Ireland held them, and held them well.

FRANCE

In George Orwell's *Animal Farm*, "all animals are equal, but some are more equal than others". Every victory is sweet, but some sweeter than others! That was certainly the case at Lansdowne Road on 19 February, 1983 when Ireland exacted revenge over France for the defeat the previous season which denied them the Grand Slam. It may not have fully compensated for that denial, but it certainly came close.

In my Cork Examiner match report I wrote: "Houdini was nothing on an Irish team which executed a near miracle comeback to maintain their challenge for the Grand Slam.''

The reference to escapism was not meant as a slight. For while Ireland gave the fans a fright at one stage, their performance was hallmarked with character. Under the stirring leadership of Ciaran Fitzgerald, they built up a comfortable 15-3 lead by half time. Then they lost the initiative — the lead — but, true to form, they hit back and France bit the dust.

Ireland dealt with a desperate late bid by the visitors with clinical efficiency. It was gripping stuff, a bruising physical contest which prompted some of the Irish players to say it was the toughest match they had ever played.

But if the big French pack just about gave them an advantage in the tight, they lost it in the loose, as the tigerish Irish won the applause of the crowd. Their spirit and speed around the field helped them overcome any problems they may have had in the set pieces and their refusal to accept defeat saw them through to a memorable victory.

The match signalled a record-breaking achievement for Ollie Campbell, who with 14 points became the most prolific scorer of all time in Irish international rugby. Those points brought his total to 169, eleven more than Tom Kiernan.

Campbell kicked Ireland ahead with a penalty after four minutes and scored another seven minutes later. Serge Blanco opened the French scoring with a penalty soon afterwards, but with Ireland doing most of the attacking, Campbell struck another and then converted a brilliant try by winger Moss Finn, the Corkman's third in international rugby.

France were far from finished though and Blanco, undoubtedly the man of the match, imposed himself on the game with an expertly created try, having already kicked his second penalty. And when he added the points to the try, France were only three points behind.

With 20 minutes left, they scored again when a little

chip behind the Irish defence caught them out and winger Esteve got over for the try.

Fitzgerald is said to have told his team: "Come on, we won the game once, let's do it again." Those words had the desired effect, because Ireland did come back, full-back Hugo MacNeill taking advantage of a French handling error to boot the ball up field, and when wing Sella went down on the ball near his own line, he was engulfed by Irishmen. MacNeill and Ringland were the first there. Kiernan was next and he passed to Duggan. Campbell, Fitzgerald and McGrath all handled before Finn was sent crashing over at the corner for his second try.

That was enough to carry the day for Ireland but Campbell made sure of victory when he kicked a penalty near the finish.

WALES

No Triple Crown. No Grand Slam. Ireland's dreams came crashing down around them at the National Stadium in Cardiff when flamboyant Wales gave them a costly lesson in the basics.

Ireland's performance, after a bright start, degenerated into one which was error-ridden and one which lacked purpose. Wales, in contrast, were highly charged and found a blend which shattered hapless Ireland.

The Cardiff bogey continued. Ireland sought their first victory there in 16 years, but as this game progressed their hopes of achieving it bordered on the impossible. Wales were spirited, aggressive and fluent. Ireland never settled, and they panicked in the face of the Welsh barrage. Gone was the confidence instilled in the Irish team after victories over Scotland and France.

Ireland held the edge for the opening 20 minutes but failed to take advantage of a clear-cut territorial advantage. But when the Welsh pack began to get on top, the ominous signs were there and the dynamic Terry Holmes, with one of his best displays ever, was man of the match, splitting

Ireland's defence with his running and inch-perfect tactical kicking. His early try, an action replay of the one in Lansdowne Road a year before, broke Irish hearts and gave Wales a grip on the game which they were never to lose.

For the first time in the season the pack, with the exception of Fitzgerald and John O'Driscoll, looked tired. The rot started and finished with the forwards even if most of the serious mistakes came from the backline — a unit under severe pressure.

Ireland got a great start when Hugo MacNeill kicked a huge penalty but they were never allowed in front for long. Mark Wyatt equalised almost immediately and when Ollie kicked a penalty Wyatt was in form again a minute later. And then came a shattering blow, when Wyatt got in for a try on the overlap and he converted himself.

If the Irish were still in the contest at half-time, immediately after the resumption it was clearly all over, for then Terry Holmes broke through the cover for a try which some deemed controversial. Elgin Rees grabbed another try seven minutes later and Campbell and Wyatt finished the scoring when they exchanged penalties. A most disappointing Irish performance, but all was not lost yet.

ENGLAND

The roar of approval by the Irish fans which greeted Tony Ward's return to international rugby at Lansdowne Road on 19 March was not a reflection on the earlier performance of Ollie Campbell, who limped off with a hamstring injury just a few minutes from time. It merely summed up the ecstasy of the supporters, who wished to tell the world — if they did not already know — that Ireland had plenty of talent on the bench.

Campbell surely did not mind, for he had already made an indelible mark on the match, scoring his first try for Ireland and contributing a total of 21 points in the 25-10 victory, giving him a total of 52 points for the season. As Campbell hobbled off, he managed a smile for Ward and a quick pat on the back. "Go in there and finish them off," one could almost hear him saying.

As it turned out, there was no time for Ward to do anything. He only got two touches of the ball, but they were enough to bring back some happy memories. England's challenge had already gone to the wall.

The Irish victory was one born out of skill and tremendous commitment. They wanted to prove that the Cardiff performance was a one-off, and they did.

The pressure on the side was great. A few weeks before, the Grand Slam which had eluded them the previous season seemed within sight, but Wales put paid to that. Yet, when they needed most to prove themselves, Ireland managed to come through. Campbell, with his impressive points total may have swung the issue, but really it was the forwards who laid the very foundation of victory.

An after-match comment by English captain, John Scott, just about summed it up: "Every one of the Irish pack thought in split seconds. We thought in seconds and just could not match them."

Irish chairman of selectors, P. J. Dwyer, quipped: "They owed us one, and boy, did they repay us!" For Dwyer, and for coach, Tom Kiernan, both at the end of their terms of office, the win, which ultimately secured Ireland a share in the championship, was a most satisfactory end to a season which might have gone sour.

Dusty Hare, so often a matchwinner for England, was responsible for the 12-10 advantage they enjoyed at the half-way stage, kicking four penalty goals to Ireland's one try and two penalties. Hare kicked his first in 12 minutes but shortly afterwards flanker Fergus Slattery drove over the line for the try, after Moss Keane had been held short. Hare found form again after 21 minutes; Ollie Campbell kicked his opening points and they exchanged penalties before Hare got his fourth before the break.

But that lead was never enough. The Irish pack, in great form, having come to grips with early scrummaging problems and having totally dominated England in the

Harry McKibbin relaxes at Kroonstaad Bowling Green, South Africa, in 1938.

The Irish contingent on the 1938 tour take time out for a photo call.

The legendary Jackie Kyle and Tom Clifford await the outcome of this tussle in 1950.

One of the greatest exponents of the dribble, Tom Clifford, shows the way to captain Karl Mullen against Otago.

No try this time for 1959 top scorer in New Zealand, Tony O'Reilly, as Bill Mulcahy watches him drive over the touchline.

Captain for the day, Andy Mulligan introduces Lord Wakefield to Noel Murphy and the rest of the team.

Mike Gibson crashes over for a try during the 1966 tour to New Zealand.

Noel Murphy getting the ball away, with Irish players Willie John McBride, Ronnie Lamont and Ray McLoughlin in the background.

Mick Doyle and Jeff Young escort the injured Roger Young off the field during a 1968 South African encounter.

Willie John McBride in action against Natal in 1968.

The Irish team which met Scotland in 1960. Ten of the players were Lions at one time or another. Back row (l. to r.): Noel Murphy, Bill Mulcaby, Gerry Culliton, Syd Millar, Gordon Wood, Cecil Pedlow. Front row (l. to r.): Tim McGrath, Dave Hewitt, Mick English, Andy Mulligan, Bert McCallan, Wally Bowman, Ronnie Kavanagh. On ground: Tom Kiernan and Jerry Walsh.

Two All Black legends, Don Clarke and Bob Scott, get in a bit of goal kicking practice — just to prove they are not past it. Notice Scott's bare foot!

Cheese! Coach Noel Murphy, John O'Driscoll and Phil Orr in happy mood in South Africa, 1980.

Willie Duggan under siege during the 1977 tour to New Zealand.

The injured David Irwin giving the thumbs up sign to his replacement, Michael Kiernan, during the 1982 Triple Crown match against Wales.

Tom Kiernan with his nephew, Michael.

John O'Driscoll smothers Terry Holmes, but the Welshman gets the ball away in the 1982 match at Lansdowne Road.

Bottoms up: Trevor Ringland touches down, unimpeded by a Gareth Davies tackle, and is immediately congratulated by a jubilant David Irwin.

Thou shalt not pass: Moss Keane lunges forward to restrain an equally determined Maurice Colclough.

English prop forward Gary Pearce under attack as Ciaran Fitzgerald and Willie Duggan prepare for the execution. And more help is on its way!

The 1982 team which beat Scotland at Lansdowne Road to clinch Ireland's first Triple Crown win since 1949.
Back row (l. to r.): Fergus Slattery, Gerry McLoughlin, John O'Driscoll, Donal Lenihan, Moss Keane, Willie Duggan, Hugo MacNeill, Phil Orr. Front row: Michael Kiernan, Paul Dean, Ollie Campbell, Ciaran Fitzgerald, J. J. Moore (IRFU president), Moss Finn, Robbie McGrath, Keith Crossan. John Murphy, David Irwin and Trevor Ringland are not included in the photo.

The artistry of Ollie Campbell in evidence as he weaves his way past Steve Pokere and Ian Dunn in the first test of the 1983 Lions New Zealand tour in Christchurch. David Irwin and Peter Winterbottom are the other Lions players.

The test front row, Graham Price, Ciaran Fitzgerald and Staff Jones, prepares to pack down yet again.

Donal Lenihan in flying form at Hawkes Bay.

Crocks' corner! Nigel Melville, Jeff Squire and Ian Stephens pose with Trevor Ringland, Jim Calder, Michael Kiernan, Graham Price and team physiotherapist, Kevin Murphy.

Allan Hewson (Wellington) with an unorthodox tackle on Michael Kiernan . . . but it did not stop a Lions try.

The rain at Carisbrook: Fitzgerald chasing All Black scrum half, Dave Loveridge.

David Irwin is watched by Trevor Ringland as he scores against South-land.

John Rutherford showing his delight after scoring a try in the third test, while Campbell prepares for the convert.

loose, were rampant. Campbell missed an early second-half penalty but then scored the try which was to smash the English spirit. Robbie McGrath chipped ahead from a scrum, Ringland raced away in pursuit and although the ball bounced unkindly for him, he managed a tap back to Campbell, who turned and then twisted his way over for the try. Campbell added the conversion and kicked penalties in the seventh and fifteenth minutes of the half. England were thereafter confined to a sporadic raid even if Ireland were never as dominant again, and while Hare kicked another penalty seven minutes from the end, Campbell, before his departure, kicked a further penalty.

THE TEAMS

IRELAND v SCOTLAND

Scotland. P. Dods (Gala), K. Robertson (Melrose), J. Renwick (Hawick), D. Johnston (Watsonians), R. Baird (Kelso), R. Wilson (London Scottish), R. Laidlaw (Jedforest), G. McGuinness (West of Scotland), C. Deans (Hawick), I. Milne (Heriots), B. Cuthbertson (Harlequins), A. Tomes (Hawick), J. Calder (Stewarts Melville), I. Paxton (Selkirk), D. Leslie (Gala).

Ireland. H. MacNeill (Oxford University), T. Ringland, (Ballymena), D. Irwin (Instonians), M. Kiernan (Dolphin), M. Finn (Constitution), O. Campbell (Old Belvedere), R. McGrath (Wanderers), P. Orr (Old Wesley), C. Fitzgerald (St Mary's, capt.), G. McLoughlin (Shannon), M. Keane (Lansdowne), D. Lenihan (Constitution), J. O'Driscoll (Manchester), W. Duggan (Blackrock), F. Slattery (Blackrock).
Referee: J. C. Yché (France).

IRELAND v FRANCE

Ireland. H. MacNeill (Oxford), T. Ringland (Ballymena),

D. Irwin (Instonians), M. Kiernan (Dolphin), M. Finn (Constitution), O. Campbell (Old Belvedere), R. McGrath (Wanderers), P. Orr (Old Wesley), C. Fitzgerald (St Mary's, capt.), G. McLoughlin (Shannon), D. Lenihan (Constitution), M. Keane (Lansdowne), F. Slattery (Blackrock), W. Duggan (Blackrock), J. O'Driscoll (Manchester).

France. S. Blanco (Biarritz), P. Sella (Agen), D. Codorniou (Narbonne), C. Belescair (Bayonne), P. Esteve (Narbonne), C. Delage (Agen), P. Berbizier (Lourdes), P. Dospital (Bayonne), B. Herrero (Nice), R. Paparamborde (Pau), J. F. Imbernon (Perpignon), J. Condom (Boucau), D. Erbani (Agen), J. L. Joinel (Brive), J. P. Rives (Racing, capt.).
Referee: A. Hosie (Scotland).

IRELAND v WALES

Wales. M. Wyatt (Swansea), E. Rees (Neath), R. Ackerman (London Welsh), D. Richards (Swansea), C. Rees (London Welsh), M. Dacey (Swansea), T. Holmes (Cardiff), S. Jones (Pontypool), B. James (Aberavon), G. Price (Pontypool), J. Perkins (do.), R. Norster (Cardiff), J. Squire (Pontypool), E. Butler (do., capt.), D. Pickering (Llanelli).

Ireland. H. MacNeill (Oxford), T. Ringland (Ballymena), D. Irwin (Instonians), M. Kiernan (Dolphin), M. Finn (Constitution), O. Campbell (Old Belvedere), R. McGrath (Wanderers), P. Orr (Old Wesley), C. Fitzgerald (St Mary's, capt.), G. McLoughlin (Shannon), D. Lenihan (Constitution), M. Keane (Lansdowne), F. Slattery (Blackrock), W. Duggan (Blackrock), J. O'Driscoll (Manchester).
Referee: J. A. Trigg (England).

IRELAND v ENGLAND

Ireland. H. MacNeill (Oxford), T. Ringland (Ballymena), D. Irwin (Instonians), M. Kiernan (Dolphin), M. Finn

(Constitution), O. Campbell (Old Belvedere), R. McGrath (Wanderers), P. Orr (Old Wesley), C. Fitzgerald (St Mary's, capt.), G. McLoughlin (Shannon), D. Lenihan (Constitution), M. Keane (Lansdowne), F. Slattery (Blackrock), W. Duggan (Blackrock), J. O'Driscoll (Manchester). Reserve: T. Ward (St Mary's) for Campbell.

England. D. Hare (Leicester), J. Carleton (Orrell), C. Woodward (Leicester), P. Dodge (Leicester), D. Trick (Bath), J. Horton (Bath), N. Youngs (Leicester), C. Smart (Newport), P. Wheeler (Leicester), G. Pearce (Northampton), S. Boyle (Gloucester), S. Bainbridge (Gosforth), N. Jeavons (Moseley), J. Scott (Cardiff, capt.), P. Winterbottom (Headingly).
Referee: J. B. Anderson (Scotland).

CHAPTER 10

DECISION DAY

On Monday 21 March, less than 48 hours after Ireland had completed their season with a win over England, I braced myself for what was to be a long work session. The Lions selectors, Willie John McBride of Ballymena and Ireland, Jim Telfer of Selkirk and Scotland, Rhys Williams of Llanelli and Wales, John Finlan of Moseley and England and Brian O'Brien of Shannon, Munster and Ireland, had made up their minds.

At precisely 11 a.m., the following Press Association message arrived in our *Cork Examiner* office: "1 Rugby Rush . . . Ciaran Fitzgerald to captain Lions in New Zealand." End rush.

The weeks and months of intense speculation about the captaincy was over. Fitzgerald had received the ultimate rugby accolade. His track record as one of Ireland's most successful captains had been rewarded. He had, over two seasons, helped to put Irish rugby back on the map and in that spell was by far the most consistent and successful leader of the four home countries.

There were those who did not want him there, and in Britain, or more specifically, in some publications in England, a campaign had been waged for Peter Wheeler to lead the side. Nobody could say anything against Peter Wheeler's playing abilities. A great hooker, he had been one of the stars of the Lions side in South Africa in 1980 and had played three times as much for his country as Fitzgerald had for his.

As a captain, Wheeler had done very well with Leicester, and this indisputably made him a very live candidate. But there were those who turned a blind eye to the fact that he was overlooked for the English captaincy, both when Billy Beaumont had been forced to retire two seasons previously, and again when the incumbent to the job, Steve Smith, lost the job the season before. Why? Only the English selectors know that.

One must have sympathy for the Englishman, for as all this was happening, England were going through a traumatic season in which they failed to win a match. His claims on the captaincy were dwindling and they finally disappeared on 19 March at Lansdowne Road when Fitzgerald led Ireland to a marvellous victory. Wheeler was in the side that day and did nothing to prove he is a better player than Fitzgerald.

Tour Manager McBride made it clear well before that March press conference that they were looking for a captain who could command a test place. The argument against Fitzgerald was that he could not. Clearly the selectors thought he could. I spoke with selector Brian O'Brien shortly before the tour departed for New Zealand. He said: "In my opinion, Fitzgerald was the only logical choice and it seems the only people who did not want him were sections of the press."

There were further shots fired against the Irishman when his side slumped to Wales. Where did that leave him? O'Brien admitted: "We had done most of our homework before that match. No selector worth his salt could have excluded him based on information from just one game. Have no doubt, the reason Fitzgerald was made captain was because he was the best at our disposal."

Fitzgerald's reaction was one of relief — that the speculation at least was over. The controversy would go on. I spoke with him on the evening of his selection and he paid particular tribute to the Irish team who, he said, were undoubtedly responsible: "When I took over the captaincy, the side was developing nicely. As a forward, I have found that the men around me have helped my own game considerably."

How would he cope with helping to mould and blend a side with players from four different countries together? Fitzgerald replied: "Pride will be the prevailing factor. I believe that any player selected from the Lions should, and will be proud to wear the jersey and will be prepared to work for one another. Sure, there will be difficulties. I accept that, but I believe the players will be Lions first, and Lions to the bitter end in New Zealand."

The selection of seven of his Irish colleagues to undertake the trip also did not really cause much surprise, either at home or across the channel. All of them — Hugo MacNeill, Trevor Ringland, David Irwin, Michael Kiernan, Ollie Campbell, Donal Lenihan and John O'Driscoll — had participated in two momentous years, two golden years of Irish rugby. While I don't wish to sound nationalistic in my view, I believe the party might well have contained more players from Ireland, for Phil Orr, Willie Duggan and Fergus Slattery, all of whom would certainly have been selected, were unavailable.

MacNeill, a post-graduate economics student at Oxford University, made his début for Ireland against France in 1981 and had, up to the tour, won 13 caps, while never being dropped. He showed tremendous form in the Triple Crown winning year and although he was prone to occasional error in the 1982/83 season, he certainly justified his retention in the Irish team and his selection for the Lions.

Some would claim the selection of Trevor Ringland was a surprise, but he always had to be in with a chance. He may not have the pace of some other international wingers, but Ringland is the type of player who uses the abilities he has got; he is a strong, determined runner who does not easily get injured, while he is also very strong in defence.

The return to international rugby of David Irwin was as much a tribute to his determination as it was to the needs of the Irish team in the centre of the field. Irwin broke his leg in the first half of Ireland's opening championship match against Wales at Lansdowne Road on 23 January 1982, in a successful bid to stop Welsh full-back Gwyn Evans from scoring. But after being forced to sit and watch Ireland successfully take their first Triple Crown in 33 years, Irwin grimly stuck to a heavy training schedule to build up the wasted muscles. He had made a successful return to rugby the previous season, and finally regained the type of form which had made him an international in the first place. He played very well for Ireland that season and his selection was completely justified.

When Irwin broke his leg, he was replaced by young Corkman Michael Kiernan who then continued to share in the Triple Crown and championship triumphs of the following two years. Like Irwin he had been on the Irish tour to South Africa in 1981 and although he did not play in the test teams, his potential was noted there, as it had been in the schools' international arena a couple of seasons before. A sprint champion, he caused problems for England, Scotland, Wales and France when he played against them and he capped a marvellous season last year with his first international try against Scotland.

If this quartet were deep in the running, an automatic choice was out-half Ollie Campbell, whose phenomenal goal-kicking success rate had brought himself and Ireland new records in the 1982/83 season. A Lion in 1980, when he played in three tests despite injury problems early in the tour, Campbell had been the scourge of the opposition and his qualities were not confined to goal-kicking. He is the complete player, a live-wire attacker and keen, often devastating tackler. Campbell was the man on whom most people relied to pose a threat to the All Blacks. Campbell made his début for Ireland in 1976 as a replacement for Barry McGann against Australia and when selected for the Irish tour to Australia in 1979 was number two to Tony Ward. There was a major controversy when he was selected for the test games but he was an instant success and if the battle between himself and Ward continued later, the old Belvederian had re-established himself as Ireland's, and possibly the world's, greatest out-half in the previous two seasons.

The holder of 22 caps for Ireland, and four times capped by the Lions in South Africa in 1980, John O'Driscoll has been a magnificent example of what a blind side flanker should be and his success is reflected in the honours bestowed upon him. The Lions always need experience, men who can say "I've been there" and O'Driscoll had. He is a tireless worker who never shirks, and the only threat to his place in the party would have been a sudden, dramatic loss of form. That just did not happen, because this man is consistently good, being responsible in a big way for Ireland's success in the two previous seasons.

On 3 May 1983, I departed from Cork airport bound for London, and from there to New Zealand, accompanied by two of the players — Kiernan and Donal Lenihan, the big second row forward whose rise to international rugby had been predictable and whose selection for the Lions was equally predictable. Lenihan was in high spirits as we set off, and again at a function held in the New Zealand High Commission later that evening. We spoke together, he, Kiernan and I, for over an hour because, he said: "Us Cork guys must stick together on this tour." The following day I made my way to the team's first run together, where the players would be subjected to fitness tests and speed trials. As we waited patiently for over an hour, I sensed that something was wrong. Then Willie John McBride walked into the ground, called the press together, and told us: "Donal Lenihan will not be travelling to New Zealand. He has returned home on medical advice to have a hernia operation. A replacement will be named later."

What a start to the tour! For Lenihan, capped nine times by Ireland, a young man who had won prized possession for his country, who had scrummaging ability beyond his years and who was developing into a player who would be around for many years to come, it must have been a sickener. His departure was a severe blow to the Lions.

The weeks went by. Lenihan had his operation and some time later a message was flashed through to the touring party management, indicating that Lenihan was again fit and ready to travel if the need arose. Nick Jeavons had already joined the tour as an additional player because of an injury to O'Driscoll, and Nigel Melville had been called upon to replace Terry Holmes. Time was slipping by fast but on 23 June the Constitution man was preparing for the second time to become a Lion. This time he would make it.

The Welsh second row, Robert Norster, who had deservedly established for himself one of the test berths, had been suffering from a back injury in the days leading up to the second test. He played in that match, but it was evident in the second half that he was struggling. He could not leave the field, because the Lions had used up one replacement — John Beattie who came in for Iain Paxton — and all they were left with was a hooker, Colin Deans, and a prop forward, Iain Milne. As the game progressed, the injury affected Norster more and he was in severe pain after the match. The problem persisted in the ensuing days, so much so that finally, on the Thursday after the match in Whangarei, he was taken to hospital for x-rays. An abnormal bone in the back was discovered and he would not be able to play for ten days to three weeks. Lenihan was called for and thus he became a fully fledged Lion, not just a one-day wonder.

Joining him on the same aircraft was another Irishman, Gerry McLoughlin of Shannon, who was being flown out to replace Ian Stephens. For the Welshman it was a tragic end to a tour to which he had given everything. Stephens had damaged knee ligaments against Southland on 11 June but had worked hard afterwards to get back into action. Having been named in the side to meet North Auckland, he was happy that he would come through to challenge for a place in the third test, but after a mere 60 seconds of training on 23 June, he broke down. McLoughlin, capped 17 times for Ireland since he first played for his country in

1979 had been on the stand-by list, one of a few players unlucky not to have made the party in the first place. Although normally a tight head prop and selected to replace a loose head, McLoughlin was a fairly logical choice because he had plenty of experience in the loose side, having played for club, province and Ireland B in that position. And so there were nine!

CHAPTER 11

FROM NORTH TO SOUTH

Wanganui, a town of some 37,000 souls on the West coast of New Zealand's North Island was the ideal centre from which to begin the tour. A peaceful and tranquil place, its people were hospitable and friendly and its second division rugby side gave the Lions a scare before collapsing and fading into oblivion. It was here that the big build-up began, with five days of intensive training, and after two days of heavy rain, the sun burst through to make the Lions stay there a most pleasant one.

WANGANUI

If anything soured the visit, it was the after-match comments by Wanganui coach, Roger Boon, and captain, Bruce Middleton. Speaking about their 47-15 defeat, Boon accused the Lions of scrummaging in an illegal manner, while Middleton was quoted as saying the Lions forwards were "soft", although the Wanganui flanker, then a contender for a place in the New Zealand side, declared later he had been misquoted. In any event, the tourists proved conclusively that they were not soft — against such opposition at least — and they handed out a fairly costly lesson to the home side, particularly to Middleton whose All Black chances literally went down the drain.

The powerful display of the pack, led superbly by captain Ciaran Fitzgerald and prompted by the brilliance of Jeff Squire, was all too much for Wanganui, who put up, nevertheless, a battling side which helped keep the game interesting for almost an hour.

It may be true to say that the Lions did not play a scintillating brand of rugby and afterwards there was some criticism of their back play. Certainly the backs did not swing the ball around with gay abandon, but then they did not always have it to do so.

When they were in possession they made some mistakes, typical of a side assembled together for the first time, but they showed flashes of genius at times as well. Two marvellous runs by Irishman Michael Kiernan, the second of which led indirectly to a try, will be remembered.

Their basic problem, and that applied to the pack also, was one of communication, but if on occasions they got their calls mixed up, the matter sorted itself out as the game wore on.

New Zealand coach Bryce Rope was at the game, and he was not of the same opinion as Boon and Middleton. He was impressed by the Lions — "despite those mistakes".

As a result of the Lions dominance in the forwards, the game was not a classic, for they elected to play it tight, and Scottish fly-half John Rutherford, instead of opening it up, invariably broke back inside to link up with the back row trio of Squire, John Beattie and Peter Winterbottom. It was a ploy which eventually paid rich dividends, unattractive though it may have been.

In fairness, the criticism of the Lions side was fairly confined. The vast majority agreed that it was a fairly good performance for a first match. The scoreline, a winning margin of 32 points, tells a lot but even that did not reflect the true scoring power of the side, for if anxiety had not been present early on, I feel certain that another 20 points could have been added.

Tribute must be paid to Wanganui for the way in which they contested the match. They led twice in the opening minutes, trailed by just seven points at half-time and then came to within a point before missing two crucial penalty chances.

It was then that the true character of the tourists came through and then that the leadership qualities of Fitzgerald became evident. His on-field team talks certainly impressed referee Lawrence who said later: "He certainly seems to have the ability to lift a side when things are going against him".

And lift them he did, for in the last 26 minutes everything finally clicked into place. The Lions scored four tries and 31 points in that spell to crush the Wanganui challenge. The early goalkicking of Wanganui full-back Tom Fearn kept the Lions under pressure. He kicked one penalty after nine minutes and, after John Rutherford dropped a goal, added another in 14 minutes.

But a minute later, the Lions got in for their first try of the tour and that honour went to Trevor Ringland. It started with a Rutherford break and after perfectly timed passes from him, Robert Ackerman and Michael Kiernan, Ringland had the pace to get outside three defenders and score in the corner.

Penalties by Dusty Hare in the eighteenth and twenty-third minutes stretched the lead to 13-6 and the full-back struck again seven minutes from the break after Fearn had kicked his third penalty for Wanganui.

The Lions might have wrapped it up before the break, with Roy Laidlaw, the Scottish scrum-half putting a foot in touch before he had sent number eight John Beattie away for a "try", and then the scrum-half himself was pulled down inches from the line after a spectacular break from 20 yards.

Instead it was Wanganui who scored next. The second half was only a minute old when young out-half Murray Kendrict tested Hare with a high ball under his own posts. Hare, possibly blinded by the sun, stood transfixed as the ball bounced in front of him, rolled on to strike the butt of an upright and came back straight into the hands of centre Shaun Crowley who dived over at the posts. Fearn converted. That Fearn missed two kickable penalties in quick succession was a source of relief to the Lions who had their worst spell in the 10 minutes immediately after half time.

But once they got themselves together again, Wanganui did not have a hope. After 14 minutes, Rutherford dropped his second goal, with Hare adding a penalty immediately. A brilliant 75-yard run by Kiernan brought play from deep inside his own half right to the Wanganui line and after a succession of scrums, Squire got in at the corner for the try which Hare converted.

Then the "floodgates" opened. Hare kicked a penalty and when Hare and Ringland combined, a second try was set up for Squire with the full-back again converting. Beattie got another after 40 minutes and in injury time Hare added the points to a Peter Winterbottom try.

The three Irishmen in the side all did well. Captain Fitzgerald made his début as a player and as a leader a winning one and played a major role in the success of the pack. As part of a rock steady scrum, his support play was noticeable on many occasions.

Kiernan was not particularly oversupplied with ball, but when he did get moving he looked the most dangerous back on view and he was certainly a little unlucky not to have scored after that explosive second-half break. Like the rest of the backline in their settling-in period, he tended at times to take too much out of it. He was singled out for honourable mention by the New Zealand press.

Trevor Ringland was, along with Dusty Hare, blamed for Wanganui's try because he was the second nearest to the ball. To my mind there can be no doubt but that the responsibility lay with Hare although an after-match discussion with an English media man suggested that in similar circumstances for England, the ball would have been covered by the winger with Hare looping around to support. Ringland otherwise had a sound game, earning the distinction of scoring the first try and helping to create another.

AUCKLAND

The failure to risk playing Maurice Colclough might well

have been responsible for the Lions losing their second game to Auckland — a match lost in the final minute of the game. Big English second row, Colclough, when eventually introduced to the team, did not reproduce the form he had shown in South Africa in 1980, but yet would likely have posed a threat to the experienced All Black duo of Andy Hayden and Garry Whetton who took second-half line-out possession just about any time they felt like it.

Colclough suffered a serious knee injury in the international championship match against France the previous January and was an extremely doubtful starter for the tour. But he battled his way back after a delicate operation which involved the removal of a cartilage and repair of ligaments and, having declared himself available, was an obvious choice.

He did not play in the opening match against Wanganui, but most expected him to line out against Auckland. While the selectors, tour manager McBride, coach Telfer and captain Fitzgerald may have had very good reasons for not playing him — and certainly he had not looked quite ready in the weeks' training prior to the first match — they did not tell anyone. Every player was available for selection according to McBride.

One should be fair, I suppose. Welshman Robert Norster was an original selection in the second row along with Steve Boyle and had he played, the Lions performance out of touch would surely have improved. Norster had stitches inserted in an ear wound during the Wanganui game and the injury caused him so much discomfort in the ensuing few days that he was pulled out and replaced by Steve Bainbridge.

I do not wish to slight the two Englishmen who marked Whetton and Hayden that afternoon, but they were quite simply not up to the task. A big, experienced campaigner was most certainly needed. The selectors gambled on holding Colclough for the third match, and they lost.

Another factor in the defeat was probably the performance of the back row, two of whom were in for their first match of the tour. A rib injury suffered by Ireland's John O'Driscoll, which forced him out of the tour for three weeks, contributed to their lack of control but so too did below par displays from John Beattie at number eight and more particularly from Jim Calder at the other side.

And so the controlled forward play, which was a distinct feature of their game in Wanganui, admittedly against much weaker opposition, was missing. The Lions pack simply ran up against a damn fine side, a side which grew in confidence as the game progressed. On a ground which was not conducive to good football, the Lions ran out of steam in the last 30 minutes, having looked very much the part of winners in the opening half.

What better way to celebrate a Centennial than with a victory over the Lions, who afterwards graciously admitted that they were beaten by a better side. Auckland may have had to wait until late in the game for out-half Grant Fox to pop over the winning points from a drop goal, but nobody in the touring party would have been in a position to say "we was robbed".

Coach Jim Telfer summed it up — "Auckland showed us up for what we were — not very good" — and that, judging their performance over the last half an hour, was being kind.

The Lions did of course play some constructive football. In fact they were on top throughout the first half, and with a little more luck and better finishing, might well have held a more handsome half-time lead than six points. But it was clear that the settling-in period had not been overcome. The first few matches are generally used as warm-up games. Against opposition the calibre of Auckland, the Lions could hardly approach it in such a manner. Here was a team ready to be scalped . . . and Auckland, national champions, were the indians. The lack of communication in a side playing for the first time, which was also evident in Spriggens Park, Wanganui, the previous Saturday, was clearly a problem, and only match practise would solve that.

144

There were some pleasing aspects, particularly from the Irish viewpoint. Full back Hugo MacNeill and David Irwin were making their Lions début. MacNeill unfortunately had to retire with a head injury early in the second half, but before that he had proved unbeatable under the high ball and his bravery was noted by an appreciative audience.

Irwin scored a magnificent try, created for him expertly by scrum-half Terry Holmes, but executed to perfection by the big Northern Ireland centre.

It would be unfair to criticise John O'Driscoll, whose injury undoubtedly hampered him, and unfair to criticise Fitzgerald either. A small section of the British media, who have consistently indulged themselves in "Fitzgerald bashing" later tried to hang the defeat on the captain's method of throwing the ball into the line-out. They completely ignored the fact that the Lions may have lost out in this facet of the game simply because the men marking big men Hayden and Whetton were not good enough. In any event, it is ludicrous to suggest that one man, unless he had made a series of appalling errors, was responsible for losing this match. Fitzgerald, in the circumstances, had a reasonably good game.

There was no doubt but that Ollie Campbell was bang on form. He, in fact, very nearly saved the game. After a first half in which his tactical kicking was a revelation, he brought off a series of super tackles as the Auckland "machine" began to reach full speed.

Apart from the failure of the tourists' pack to impose themselves on the game, the biggest single disappointment was the performance of Clive Woodward in the centre. Woodward is a player for whom I have the utmost admiration, but he did not have a happy season before being chosen for the tour. His first game was a bad start for him and apart from being hesitant in defence, a lack of pace was glaringly obvious at one period of the first half when he hacked the ball through the Auckland defence and a score looked certain. Amazingly, however, the home right-winger, John Kirwin, was able to come right across the pitch and beat him to the touchdown.

A few minutes later, Grant Fox opened the scoring with a penalty goal. The Lions however struck back and Campbell, after dropping a goal, converted Irwin's try before MacNeill struck a mammoth penalty from the half-way line.

Fox narrowed the gap near half-time with a penalty and eight minutes after the resumption Auckland set up a try from deep inside their own half after Woodward was tackled and dispossessed. Gary Cunningham was the scorer after Joe Stanley had made the break. After that it was all Auckland but a gritty defence by the Lions kept them in the match until finally, Fox crushed them with that drop goal. Those points gave Auckland their second win over a Brittish and Irish side, and their first since 1930.

BAY OF PLENTY

As we arrived at our hotel in Rotorua, the centre for the next game, our bus driver warned us: "When you get a smell, for goodness sake don't stare at the nearest human being. It's only sulphur."

He was referring to the geysers which abound in and around this holiday centre, which has a year-round population of almost 50,000 people. It reminded me somewhat of a verse from the song "The Boys Of Fairhill", when poor old Father Matthew is referred to. One thing is sure, he never had to endure as bad a smell from the River Lee.

The Lions were not bothered by this, though, for on Saturday 21 May at the Rotorua International Stadium they recorded a fine victory over Bay of Plenty. They bounced into a 22 points lead in as many minutes, hit "a valley period" when Bay of Plenty cut the deficit to 10 points, but then came back to emphasise the control they had shown for much of the game.

The match marked the return to activity of Colclough and he added vital stability to the scrum, stability which was lacking against Auckland. The home side had their moments which won them widespread approval but they could not control the Lions, who, despite making mistakes and despite failing to find a midfield blend, moved extremely well at times.

There was a lack of "oomph" from England's Clive Woodward who was not shaping up to the standards everyone knows he is capable of setting himself. As a result, the Lions suffered some agonising moments for a spell after half-time when the Grant Batty-motivated Bay of Plenty backs set the scene for what might have been an amazing comeback.

The game was not without its controversy. Just as against Wanganui, there were some ugly scenes early in the game when both sides lost sight of the fact that they had come to play rugby. Two nasty brawls erupted which forced referee Colin Cregan of Waikato to bring the sides together and issue a general warning.

His intervention worked, for there were no further scenes, but after-match comments by Bay of Plenty coach Graeme Crossman evoked a firm reaction from Willie John McBride. Crossman said he had anticipated trouble, indicating that the Lions would start something. McBride replied: "We have not come here to be intimidated."

Judging from the reaction of the Lions players when the feud began, the infamous "99" call introduced by McBride's 1974 tour party in South Africa, was reintroduced. As captain of the Lions nine years ago, he and his team raced in as one whenever fighting broke out, thereby reducing the element of risk that anyone would be sent off. After all, a referee can hardly send off a whole team!

Fortunately, though, the remainder of the game flowed without incident and when the tourists got down to the serious task of rugby, there can be no doubt that they won hands down.

Bay of Plenty's failure was due, according to Crossman, to their inability to adapt to that level of rugby until it was too late. He was right, for the Lions coasted 22 points clear, but although Crossman would like to think his side matched the Lions for class later, I would disagree. They were no more than an average side whose fightback was created from spirit more than anything else, although a few players — full-back Alisdair Sutherland, centre Darrell Shelford and out-half Ron Preston — did impress me particularly. As for All Black challenger Hika Reid, he lost five strikes to Colin Deans, but everywhere else was brilliant. Those four, and captain Graeme Elvin, were about the best that could be offered by way of a serious challenge to the Lions, who were seven points up within three minutes.

Whoever suggested the touring side's backline could not score tries must have been disappointed when John Carleton finished off a wonderful movement in the left-hand corner. Dusty Hare had kicked the Lions ahead with a penalty goal after two minutes, but then second row Steve Bainbridge exposed a major weakness in the home pack when he darted through to pick up a tap back in a line-out and thunder down the right hand touchline. He was checked after 45 yards but found Iain Paxton in support. The Lions won the ruck and when Robert Ackerman was sent away he threw out a long pass to Hare who had right-wing Carleton inside him — a wonderful piece of support play from Carleton.

A quarter of an hour later, the Lions dominance in the line-outs again bore fruit. Paxton tapped down at the back to Calder and the flanker found Ian Stephens on his right, the prop forward marking his début by charging over for the try which Hare converted.

The full-back was certainly in kicking form, adding a penalty after 20 minutes and then slotting over another conversion after Ireland's Trevor Ringland went over for the third try. That score came after Sutherland had been swallowed up by the Lions centre, Woodward and Ackerman; the ruck was won and Laidlaw and Carleton had combined to split the defence on the blind side. Ringland, playing out of position on the left wing, received the pass ten yards out and crashed over in the corner.

Bay of Plenty were lucky to survive further pressure

before and after half-time, just before they themselves hit a purple patch. They ran at the Lions from everywhere and eight minutes after resumption of play, winger John Cameron sliced through the midfield defence to score near the posts. Preston converted and then scored himself after dummying and side-stepping his way past the cover. He added the points to that too, and the Lions looked in serious trouble. They knew it and the crowd knew it as they roared on their side.

But Carleton put a stop to that with his second try which came after they opened up inside their own half and after Rutherford, Iain Milne, Jeff Squire and Woodword had all handled. Hare converted and the Lions were safe.

Bay of Plenty did come back to score a soft try with eight minutes remaining but by then their aspirations of a victory had been banished. Winger Cameron got the try after Ringland had failed, according to the referee, to ground the ball behind his own line. It was a disappointing moment for Ringland, who had looked sharp early in the first half, but who, as the game went on, seemed to be suffering a crisis of confidence, with his handling and running less than acceptable.

For Bay of Plenty it did no more than put a more respectable look on the scoreline, for the Lions charged on and with four minutes left, a called moved from the back of the scrum culminated with Paxton diving in near the posts. Hare converted to finish the match with a personal tally of 14 points, bringing his two-match total to 35.

WELLINGTON

Three spectacular second-half tries and the courage displayed by the Lions in coming from behind four times during the game, were the main talking points after their 27-19 victory over Wellington at Athletic Park, an encounter which thrilled the 30,000 crowd.

The Lions trailed three times in the first half and were behind at the break. Wellington stretched their lead early in the second, lost it, regained it, and lost it again as the tourists swept to a memorable victory thanks to Ireland's Michael Kiernan and Ollie Campbell.

Three All Blacks selectors were there to watch prospective internationals and to study a Lions which was very close to the test combination. But they must have left a very confused group. That was because the Lions first half performance was one they would like to have forgotten rather quickly. In trouble up front, their scrummaging was solid but they failed to win decent possession out of touch and Wellington were very much faster to the loose ball.

At times in that period it looked as if Wellington would sweep them aside with ease as their forwards won valuable ball and a backline, packed with internationals, drove forward in a series of attacks.

That they held a mere three-point lead at the break is a tribute in itself to the Lions defence — particularly in midfield where David Irwin and Michael Kiernan provided the most potent and stable centre partnership.

And in the end, their first half showing, when mainly confined to defence, was to have even more serious consequences for Wellington, because eventually they ran out of steam. Having failed to make the vital breakthrough then, they became frustrated and disorganised and although an early second-half try was set up for winger Bernie Fraser, the Lions backline were to outscore them three to one.

It was perhaps significant that four of the backline were Irish, with Kiernan and Irwin having already played through an international campaign together. Irwin does not always get credit for the amount of work which he engages himself in but he certainly did on this occasion. The two midfield men, Ollie Campbell and Hugo MacNeill, in addition to the speedy Scottish left-winger Roger Baird, ensured that this was the best backline performance of the tour to date.

Wellington may have had players such as Allan Hewson, Stu Wilson, Jamie Salmon, Bernie Fraser and Tu Wyllie, five All Blacks whose attacking capabilities were never in question, but whose defence, in the face of magnificent support play by the Lions was eventually in serious doubt.

Roger Baird brutally exposed Michael Clamp with two tremendous runs which led to scores and Kiernan's pace and strength against Fraser was equally successful when getting in for the match-winning try near the end of the game. Considering the fact that three of that Wellington unit, Hewson, Wilson and Fraser, were later to be selected for the first test, the Lions backline performance seemed an optimistic omen.

And they won without right-winger John Carleton, who retired with concussion in the first half, and without Terry Holmes, who was victim of a kick in the head midway through the first half.

Yet there were times when victory looked impossible, particularly early in the second half when Wellington, having held a 9-6 half-time lead jumped further ahead with a Fraser try, created for him by a Hewson chip through the defence near the line. Hewson had kicked two penalties and dropped a goal in the opening half, to two penalties by Campbell.

But by the time Fraser had scored, the Lions had begun to settle. In fact that try was completely against the run of play and the tourists finally reaped the reward for intense pressure in the seventeenth minute of the second half. Roy Laidlaw, a brilliant deputy for Holmes, started it all by changing direction and linking up with Jeff Squire and Robert Norster. The big Welsh second row powered his way past several defenders and when checked, threw out an overhead pass to Kiernan, with the centre timing his pass perfectly to Baird who raced in at the corner for a try which Campbell converted.

Ten minutes from time, the Lions took the lead for the first time. Captain Ciaran Fitzgerald made the initial thrust, setting up a ruck from which Laidlaw speedily delivered to Campbell and the out-half was outside Irwin to send Kiernan away. Kiernan was tipped by a defender but as he fell to the ground he found Baird to his left and the winger jubilantly went over for his second try, with Campbell again converting.

A lapse in concentration nearly cost the Lions the game, though, for they allowed Wellington to get back at them; and when they lost a scrum five yards out, scrum-half Neil Sorenen broke left and with a short reverse pass found flanker and captain Paul Quinn who got in for the try which Hewson converted to regain the lead.

But Kiernan eventually shattered their challenge. With two minutes of normal time remaining, Norster got clear and fed Campbell, and after an orthodox backline movement, Kiernan came up to support Baird on the outside, cutting in and then using his shoulder to dispense with Hewson before his momentum carried him over the line. Campbell converted and he provided the last blow, kicking an injury-time penalty.

MANAWATU

"Licensed thuggery" was how incidents in the ensuing match against Manawatu were described by former All Black, John Graham. 23 times capped by New Zealand between 1958 and 1964 Graham called on coaches, administrators and referees to put a stop to brutality.

The Lions won, but a number of their players, Ciaran Fitzgerald, Iain Paxton and Graham Price in particular, had been subjected to a series of kicks to the upper body and head by "over-spirited" Manawatu forwards.

The after-match press conference was something of a joke. Manawatu coach, Graham Hamer who in a pre-match interview had made all sorts of allegations about the Lions' way of playing the game, claiming that they had been responsible for any fights in their previous games, declared: "It was a good, clean match."

It was far from that, but a re-enactment of the type of tactics Manawatu had used against the 1977 Lions, when uproar once again broke out after touring players had been assaulted.

McBride was clearly irked: "Players in our part of the world would be sent off the field for such offences. Kicking is not part of the game. I realise full well that there are different attitudes to rucking in New Zealand. I am not complaining about players being rucked out of the way but I do most strenuously object to players being kicked in the head and body," he said.

And such incidents did occur. Fitzgerald was injured four times during the match, each time the victim of a kick. His head, upper body and thighs were torn and scraped. Paxton had stitches inserted in two head wounds, and Price and others also had treatment for similar, although lesser, injuries. Later Fitzgerald branded the aggressors as cowards. "Any man who kicks another on the ground can only be termed a coward," he said.

National coach Bryce Rope and former player Colin Meads entered the debate too, but while they could not condone action of this type, Rope said the Lions, and Fitzgerald in particular, had been guilty of lying on the ball. Meads described McBride's reaction as "playing tactics before the first test."

But Graham, a headmaster at Auckland Grammar School, was quite vociferous in his condemnation. He said the administrators should act..

> We pay a lot of lip service to stamping out dirty play but the only way to stop it is to take action against offenders. The Lions do tend to pull their bodies over secondary phase ball if they cannot win it themselves. In that case they have to expect a certain amount of rucking, but only if the traditional methods are used.
>
> There is no way that stamping on heads should be tolerated and no way that this kind of thing has a part to play in sport. It is licensed thuggery and it is nonsense to suggest that the players involved had been going for the ball.
>
> A ball is a brown leather object which is quite

different from a head. Good players do not ruck with their eyes shut and they should know exactly what they are putting their feet on.

So that was the after-match scene, but if the Lions were battered and bruised, they were generally quite a happy group. It was their third victory in succession and it helped to erase the memory of that defeat by Auckland.

Manawatu, purely from the rugby angle, were quite a strong side and the Lions did not have it easy — not by a long shot. A fiercely partisan home crowd gave some of the Lions a hard time of it, sometimes for even the most inconsequential errors. In the immediate pre-match build-up, a song "Lion Taming Day" blared over the public address system, as if to whet the crowd's appetite.

Many of the players came in for verbal abuse from that crowd and Scottish scrum-half Roy Laidlaw came in for more than his share. Laidlaw had, in contrast to his earlier performances, a poor game and that crowd certainly let him know it. Another object of scorn was Ireland's Trevor Ringland who, after dropping one pass early in the game, was also singled out. But Ringland had the last laugh, for after scoring a super try early in the second half, he sealed the issue with another nine minutes from the end — at a time when the Lions had been trailing 15-18.

Manawatu began brightly and within four minutes out-half Matene Love dropped a goal, with Mark Finlay sending a penalty wide just afterwards. The Lions deservedly got back into it when Fitzgerald was blown over by a defender, the ball not anywhere near him. Campbell kicked the resultant penalty.

But Finlay was to restore the home lead after 27 minutes when he dropped a goal after Laidlaw failed to find touch, and the Manawatu full-back kicked an injury-time penalty to give his side a six points half-time lead.

The Lions, and Ringland in particular, set the scene for an absorbing if sometimes disturbing second half. Ollie Campbell broke in midfield, found Hugo MacNeill outside him and the full-back sent Ringland away. The winger cut inside and then outside again before speeding away to get in near the corner and Campbell added the points from a difficult angle.

Referee Dave Bishop made a remarkable error in judgement in penalising the Lions under their own posts a minute later. Video film later confirmed that Fitzgerald was stamped upon by a Manawatu forward but when Robert Norster made a vain bid to retaliate with his fist, he was the one found guilty of committing an offence. Mr Bishop said later he did not see it, and that may be so, but one of his linesmen must have, and failed to bring it to his attention, although he had taken more than a passing interest in other more minor incidents.

Finlay had no difficulty in slotting that one over, but Campbell kicked penalties in the thirteenth and seventeenth minutes of the second half to give the Lions the lead, before they lost it again. MacNeill failed to hold a punt through in the twenty-first minute and although he got back to save the danger, Manawatu forced three scrums in succession with scrum-half Mark Donaldson breaking from the third chipping through and finding Finlay there to dive in for the try which he converted himself.

The home crowd were obviously delighted, but they were to be shocked ten minutes later when Ringland struck. He kicked deep into the Manawatu half and when Finlay gathered, he steadied himself for the clearance. He took too long however, for Ringland blocked it down, controlled the ball and then ran in for the try near the posts which Campbell converted.

Iain Paxton gave them breathing space with a try after a scrum on the Manawatu line and although the home team made a brave comeback bid, it was the Lions who came closest to scoring, Finlay just finding touch as Kiernan blew him over.

MID CANTERBURY

Ashburton is a neat little hamlet an hour's drive away from

Christchurch which was the scene of the first test; but the Tuesday prior to that game turned out to be very forgettable. The Lions continued their winning run with a 26-6 victory over Mid Canterbury, but with only four of the test side in action they stumbled their way through against a side which was, honestly, very poor.

The only real consolation the Lions could have had was to look back to the series winning team of 1971 when they too struggled against the Combined Hanan Shield Districts of which Mid Canterbury were a party.

The Lions simply did not play well, despite the fact that they dominated the forward exchanges right throughout the game, crushing the opposition in the set scrums where loose head-prop John McLay was in severe trouble. The New Zealander later quipped: "My head is definitely closer to my behind after that experience. I've never felt so mangled in all my life," he said, after tangling with the "Bear", Iain Milne.

Again the Lions management team of McBride and more particularly Telfer, were not happy with the refereeing of Rex Soppet (Counties). Telfer's grouse was that the Lions were never able to impose themselves due to the frequency of collapsed scrums resorted to by Mid Canterbury. I am inclined to agree with Telfer to a point, for the home side were under severe pressure throughout the match and I have no doubt that the tourists would have won a much greater supply against the head were it not for many scrums being dragged down. But in fairness to Mid Canterbury and to referee Mr Soppet, I wonder was it always their fault? The strength of the Lions scrum was such that the home side could not cope and the question to be asked was whether they dropped the scrums deliberately or whether they just buckled under the strain. Telfer did raise a giggle or two though when he said: "I thought we did quite well at times — to keep them up."

But yet, for much of the game at least, the Lions failed to hammer home that advantage. They led by four points at half-time, a small enough lead considering they had the benefit of the wind in the first half, and having come safely through a gallant bid by Mid Canterbury for a score immediately after half-time, they held the edge territorially but took a long time to convert their superiority into scores. It was only as the game rolled into the third quarter that they scored a try which put them firmly in command, and even then, they squandered some chances.

The Irishmen, two in number, did well though, with Trevor Ringland playing a big role in two of the three tries, his defence rock solid and his confidence obviously back to normal after a poor display on the left wing against Bay of Plenty. Irwin set himself up for a test place, too, with another faultless display of strong running and capable defensive work.

Dusty Hare made some opportune incursions into the backline which was excellently served by Terry Holmes, but generally the backline tended to kick away possession too often, with John Rutherford and Clive Woodward the main offenders. With the pack attempting to keep the ball at close quarters too often, it did not add up to an exciting performance. The important thing of course is that they won, and on the scoreline, comfortably.

Hare gave them a great start when he kicked a penalty goal after eight minutes, but Mid Canterbury full-back Murray Holmes equalised with a penalty two minutes later and then replied to another by Hare (13 mins.) after 17 minutes.

Apart from one penalty chance to Holmes, it was all the Lions after that, with Rutherford missing two drop goals, Hare missing two penalty goals and Ringland being pushed into touch near the line after a good run. But the pressure finally told, and when a scrum was won on the home line, Holmes broke blind, found Ringland and although the Irishman was crash-tackled, he managed to get the ball away to Jim Calder, and the flanker scored.

That lead might have been eroded but for a desperate tackle on hard-running Mid Canterbury centre, Murray McLeod, three minutes into the second half and had not

Holmes been wide with a penalty kick just afterwards.

But again the challenge faded away after a bright start and in 16 minutes Hare kicked a penalty. Ringland almost got in for a superb try just afterwards but then helped set one up for Gwyn Evans which was speedily followed by another from Terry Holmes. Hare converted and with the last kick of the game, kicked a penalty.

THE FIRST TEST

The announcement of the team to meet New Zealand in the first test was greeted with some surprise. The team sheet did not contain the name of Irishman Michael Kiernan. I recall speaking to several prominent rugby commentators and supporters from both Britain, Ireland and New Zealand and the general feeling was that the selectors had erred. In the five nations championship the trend was to play left- and right-centre threequarters, but coach Jim Telfer introduced David Irwin and Robert Ackerman as his tour inside-centres, with Michael Kiernan and Clive Woodward acting as outside men.

Various combinations were used in the six games leading up to the test but the feeling was that Irwin and Kiernan had been the most successful. They played together in the match against Wellington and for the first time the Lions backline showed their real potential. And so the prediction was that while Irwin may have to fight off the challenge from the competent Ackerman for the inside position, Kiernan had done more than enough to justify his selection outside.

As it turned out, Irwin was chosen, but when Ackerman's name was read out by manager Willie John McBride, the press corps were bemused, almost stunned. The non-selection of Kiernan represented to most a negative attitude to the game. Had he not shown more flair than the Welsh-man, more pace than any of the others? Kiernan could have felt very sorry for himself, but he took the news well after the obvious initial disappointment. He said: "The selectors have every right to choose the team they think is best. I respect that right. Anyway, there is a long way to go yet."

During the build-up to the test, many more comments were to be passed regarding the selection of the mid-field men. One New Zealand rugby writer wrote: "Kiernan's exclusion seems an incredible mistake. He is the one centre who looked capable of causing real problems for the All Blacks. The Lions may well regret he will not be there."

And how true that statement turned out, for the fluency with which the backline moved in the Wellington game, due to the understanding between Campbell, Irwin, Kiernan and Scotland's Roger Baird, was missing. It would be wrong to say Ackerman played badly. He did not. He tackled soundly, but he lacked the speed and agility needed to create difficulties for the New Zealanders, and having played all his tour rugby as an inside player, took a long time — too long — to adjust to his new role. One can only look back with regret on a chance he got to score late in the first half when the sides were locked in equality. Ackerman was sent away on the blind side and with a yawning gap opened in the All Black defence, he had Trevor Ringland outside him. Ackerman tried to charge his way over but was stopped on the line; the chance was lost and so a golden opportunity went a-begging. Everyone agreed that Kiernan, in the same situation, would have gone in for the try without a hand being laid on him.

From the Lions' point of view, this was a game of lost opportunities. In the week preceding the game, bookmakers had been giving odds of five to one and more on a Lions win. "The All Blacks Set to Flatten Lions," screamed one newspaper headline.

Yet I was not really pessimistic. Apart from the Kiernan blunder, the team was as good as one could have expected. Hugo MacNeill had done enough to justify his inclusion before the spirited Englishman, Dusty Hare. Trevor Ringland had experienced one bad game — on the left wing against Bay of Plenty — but had gone on to regain his confidence, and with the experienced John Carleton out of contention, through injury, was the logical choice on the right wing. Roger Baird and Irwin had shown some excellent form, with Terry Holmes and Ollie Campbell the automatic choices at half-back. Campbell was quickly establishing himself as the player of the tour from every point of view, particularly with his goalkicking, having slotted over 12 of his 14 attempts in three matches. Ian Stephens had done just about enough to win a place in the front row alongside captain Fitzgerald and Graham Price. Maurice Colclough, Robert Norster, Jeff Squire, Iain Paxton and Peter Winterbottom were all automatic choices — all experienced internationals.

It would be true to say that the Lions had never reached their full potential for the duration of any of the six provincial matches. But they had played brilliantly at times and that, to me at any rate, suggested they could defeat the All Blacks — if everything fell into place. That they failed is now history, but it is well worth recording that it was a game they could easily have won, maybe should have won. The four points winning margin is a little flattering, for the home side scored in the very last minute with an Allan Hewson drop goal. Campbell, from behind his own line in the dying seconds, knew he had to keep the ball in play if they were to have a chance to overcome a one-point deficit.

He cleared his line with a huge diagonal kick with the express aim of having his backline chase it and hopefully get there before the All Black defence. But Hewson had read the situation, and came in to catch the clearance, steady himself and drop the goal. Nobody, but nobody, would blame Campbell for taking that risk. It was a calculated gamble which was either to come off or not. In this instance, it did not.

New Zealand were lucky to go into a 1-0 series lead, and they knew it. None more than captain Andy Dalton, one of the real nice guys of New Zealand rugby. Dalton had the unenviable task of succeeding Graham Mourie as All

Black captain, even if he had led his country before. He was generous in his praise of the Lions: "Boy, did they give us some game. It was much harder than we expected. The Lions' forwards competed very well. We struggled, especially at the back of the line-out. The ball we got was not very good. We were looking for two-handed takes but they did not eventuate. You have to give credit to them. It was not as if we played poorly. They just kept us on defence."

Big second row Andy Hayden, who at 32 was described as "one of the oldies" in the All Black side — that would raise a laugh or two from Moss Keane — was equally generous in his praise of the Lions: "This test was one of the more physically sapping contests I have been involved in. The Lions' forwards resembled more of an all Black pack in their driving, ball winning and running off each other. I was very impressed with the Lions."

Impressed he may have been, but that was no consolation to the Lions, whose utter frustration at having failed was clearly mirrored in the faces of the players. Captain Fitzgerald was obviously the most disappointed of all. He had come in for enough criticism from some quarters to last him a lifetime. Nothing would have been more satisfying to him than a win in this first test. It was not to be, but to his credit he remained calm. On Sunday morning I made my way to the team hotel, the Russley, on the outskirts of Christchurch to enquire about the extent of a knee injury suffered by Welsh scrum-half Terry Holmes the previous afternoon. The news was not good. He had torn knee ligaments and would not play again on the tour. A replacement, Nigel Melville, as yet uncapped for England at senior level, was being sent for. Melville had just returned as captain of the English B team from a highly successful tour of Romania, and was match fit, so he got the call up before Steve Smith, who had been on stand by.

It was a beautiful sunny day and most of the players sat outdoors by the swimming pool. Fitzgerald approached me and asked: "How's the book going?" We chatted for a few minutes and it was heartening to hear him say: "Whatever about being beaten, this game has given us all tremendous confidence. We now know what we are capable of."

There were a couple of reasons why the Lions lost. They failed to take their chances — and they had many in the second quarter of the game — and the All Blacks' try, scored 17 minutes into the second half, was one which to my mind should not have been allowed by referee Francis Palmade.

In their best spell of play, the Lions made several brave bids for a try which was to elude them. After 26 minutes a great forward drive was stopped only inches from the line. In 31 minutes Ackerman took the wrong option and he too was stopped. In 33 minutes Irwin gathered a kick ahead from substitute scrum-half Roy Laidlaw and drove over the line, but referee Palmade did not award a try. A minute later, Campbell sent a drop goal just wide and then Fitzgerald was held short after Winterbottom had had the initial thrust from the back of a line-out.

Campbell had kicked a penalty and dropped a goal to two penalty goals by Allan Hewson and instead of jumping in front with a try, the Lions had to be happy with a half-time lead of 9-6, with the Lions' pressure finally paying off just before the break when Campbell kicked a penalty after All Black second row Gary Whetton was penalised.

But eleven minutes into the second half, Fitzgerald wandered offside in a ruck while Hewson kicked the 45-yard goal and the All Blacks took the lead six minutes later. The ball was swept out of the backline to winger Stu Wilson and it was his pass inside to Warwick Taylor which was the major talking point. To me, it was clearly forward, but the movement was allowed to develop; and when the All Blacks won a subsequent ruck they went left, with winger Bernie Fraser being tackled by Ringland but losing the ball which Mark Shaw picked up to dive over and score.

That blow might well have killed off the Lions, but they kept plugging away and Campbell gave them renewed hope when he kicked a penalty after Taylor had obstructed

Irwin. In a great finish, MacNeill slipped as he attempted a drop goal and the ball went wide, while Campbell very nearly breached the home defence with a dazzling run. But it was the New Zealanders who provided the last bit of pressure and the last score. The Lions won the scrum on their own line, but Hewson fielded Campbell's infield kick and scored with a drop goal.

FIRST MATCH: WANGANUI
Spriggens Park, Wanganui, 14 May
Attendance: 14,000. Weather: sunny, calm. Pitch: firm.

Lions 47 (J. Squire 2 tries, T. Ringland, J. Beattie, P. Winterbottom 1 try each, D. Hare 5 penalties, 3 conversions, J. Rutherford 2 drop goals).
Wanganui 15 (S. Crowley 1 try, T. Fearn 3 penalties, 1 conversion).

Lions: D. Hare, T. Ringland, R. Ackerman, M. Kiernan, G. Evans, J. Rutherford, R. Laidlaw, S. Jones, C. Fitzgerald, (capt.), I. Milne, S. Boyle, R. Norster, J. Squire, J. Beattie, P. Winterbottom.

Wanganui: T. Fearn, D. Brooks, S. Crowley, S. Gordon, M. O'Connell, M. Kendrict, A. Donald, B. Dallison, L. Graham, R. Kahakaka, M. Wild, G. Coleman, P. Stratton, R. Parsons, B. Middleton (capt.).
Referee: K. Lawrence (Bay of Plenty).

Lions Record against Wanganui and District Sides
1930: Lions 19, Wanganui 3.
1950: Lions 31, Wanganui 3.
1959: Lions 9, Wanganui 6.
1966: Wanganui/King Country 12, Lions 6.
1971: Lions 22, Wanganui/King Country 9.
1977: Lions 60, Wanganui/King Country 9.
1983: Lions 47, Wanganui 15.

Eden Park, Auckland, 18 May.
*Attendance: 46,000. Weather: showery, windy.
Pitch: soft with muddy patches.*

Lions 12 (D. Irwin 1 try, O. Campbell 1 drop goal, 1 conversion, H. MacNeill 1 penalty).
Auckland 13 (G. Cunningham 1 try, G. Fox 2 penalties, 1 drop goal).

Lions: H. MacNeill, J. Carleton, D. Irwin, C. Woodward, R. Baird, O. Campbell, T. Holmes, S. Jones, C. Fitzgerald (capt.), G. Price, S. Bainbridge, S. Boyle, J. O'Driscoll, J. Beattie, J. Calder. Reserve: G. Evans for MacNeill.

Auckland: D. Halligan, J. Kirwin, J. Stanley, M. Mills, G. Cunningham, G. Fox, T. Burcher, J. Drake, K. Boyle, G. Burgess, G. Whetton, A. Hayden, A. Whetton, G. Rich, A. Harvey (capt.).
Referee: G. Harrison (Wellington).

Lions Record against Auckland
1930: Auckland 19, Lions 6.
1950: Lions 32, Auckland 9.
1959: Lions 15, Auckland 10.
1966: Lions 12, Auckland 6.
1971: Lions 19, Auckland 12.
1977: Lions 34, Auckland 15.
1983: Auckland 13, Lions 12.

THIRD MATCH: BAY OF PLENTY
Rotorua International Stadium, 21 May
Attendance: 34,500. Weather: fine. Pitch: firm.

Lions 34 (J. Carleton 2 tries, T. Ringland, I. Stephens, I. Paxton, 1 try each, D. Hare 4 conversions, 2 penalties).
Bay of Plenty 16 (J. Cameron, 2 tries, R. Preston 1 try, 2 conversions).

Lions: D. Hare, J. Carleton, G. Woodward, R. Ackerman, T. Ringland, J. Rutherford, R. Laidlaw, I. Stephens, C. Deans, I. Milne, M. Colclough, S. Bainbridge, J. Squire (capt.), I. Paxton, J. Calder.

Bay of Plenty: A. Sutherland, J. Cameron, D. Shelford, B. McKillop, J. Hanley, R. Preston, M. Basham, S. McDowell, H. Reid, B. Cameron, A. de Jager, G. Braid, T. Hohneck, G. Elvin (capt.), C. Ross.
Referee: C. Cregan (Waikato).

Lions Record against Bay of Plenty and District
1930: Lions 25, Bay of Plenty/Poverty Bay/East Coast 11.
1950: Lions 27, Bay of Plenty/Poverty Bay/East Coast 3.
1959: Lions 26, Bay of Plenty/Thames Valley 24.
1966: Lions 6, Bay of Plenty 6.
1971: Lions 20, Bay of Plenty 14.
1977: Lions 23, Bay of Plenty 16.
1983: Lions 34, Bay of Plenty 16.

FOURTH MATCH: WELLINGTON
Athletic Park, Wellington, 25 May.
Attendance: 30,000. Weather: cloudy. Pitch: good.

Lions 27 (R. Baird 2 tries, M. Kiernan 1 try, O. Campbell 3 penalties, 3 conversions).
Wellington 19 (B. Fraser and P. Quinn 1 try each, A. Hewson 2 penalties, 1 drop goal and 1 conversion).

Lions: H. MacNeill, J. Carleton, M. Kiernan, D. Irwin, R. Baird, O. Campbell, T. Holmes, S. Jones, C. Fitzgerald (capt.), G. Price, M. Colclough, R. Norster, J. Squire, J. Beattie, P. Winterbottom. Reserve: G. Evans for Carleton.

Wellington: A. Hewson, M. Clamp, S. Wilson, J. Salmon, B. Fraser, T. Wyllie, N. Sorensen, B. McGratten, S. Bryan, S. Crichton, G. Wilkinson, D. Archer, P. Quinn (capt.), M. Mexted, G. Duffy.

Referee: T. Doocey (Canterbury).

Lions Record against Wellington
1930: Wellington 12, Lions 8.
1950: Lions 12, Wellington 6.
1959: Lions 21, Wellington 6.
1966: Wellington 20, Lions 6.
1971: Lions 47, Wellington 9.
1977: Lions 13, Wellington 6.
1983: Lions 27, Wellington 19.

FIFTH MATCH: MANAWATU
Showgrounds Oval, Palmerston North, 28 May
Attendance: 17,000. Weather: fine but strong wind.
Pitch: firm.

Lions 25 (T. Ringland 2 tries, I. Paxton 1 try, O. Campbell 2 penalties, 2 conversions, 1 drop goal).
Manawatu 18 (M. Finlay 1 try, 1 conversion, 2 penalties, 1 drop goal, M. Love 1 drop goal).

Lions: H. MacNeill, T. Ringland, M. Kiernan, R. Ackerman, R. Baird, O. Campbell, R. Laidlaw, I. Stephens, C. Fitzgerald (capt.), G. Price, M. Colclough, R. Norster, J. Squire, I. Paxton, P. Winterbottom.

Manawatu: M. Finlay, P. McElhinney, P. Drury, I. Wood, K. Granger, M. Love, M. Donaldson, G. Knight, B. Hemara, T. Clare, F. Oliver, M. Rosenbrook, M. Shaw, G. Old, G. Grant.
Referee: D. Bishop (Southland).

Lions Record against Manawatu and District Sides
1930: Lions 34, Manawhenua 8.
1950: Lions 13, Manawatu/Horowhenua 8.
1959: Lions 26, Manawatu/Horowhenua 6.
1966: Lions 17, Manawatu/Horowhenua 8.
1971: Lions 39, Manawatu/Horowhenua 6.

1977: Lions 18, Manawatu/Horowhenua 12.
1983: Lions 25, Manawatu 18.

Ashburton Showgrounds, 31 May.
Attendance: 11,000. Weather: cool, with drizzle.
Pitch: soft.

Lions 26 (J. Calder, G. Evans, T. Holmes 1 try each,
D. Hare 4 penalties, 1 conversion).
Mid Canterbury 6 (M. Holmes 2 penalties).

Lions: D. Hare, T. Ringland, D. Irwin, C. Woodward,
G. Evans, J. Rutherford, T. Holmes, S. Jones, C. Deans,
I. Milne, M. Colclough (capt.), S. Bainbridge, N. Jeavons,
J. Beattie, J. Calder.

Mid Canterbury: M. Holmes, P. McLay, J. Mudgway,
M. McLeod, G. Frew, M. Roulston, P. Williams, J. McLay,
G. Perry (capt.), H. Gordon, J. Ross, A. Hill, A. Morrison,
P. Cunneen, W. Frew.
Referee: R. Soppet (Counties).

Lions Record against Mid Canterbury and District Sides
1930: Lions 16, Combined Hanan Shield Districts 9.
1950: Lions 29, Ashburton County/North Otago 6.
1959: Lions 21, Combined Hanan Shield Districts 11.
1966: Lions 20, Combined Hanan Shield Districts 12.
1971: Lions 25, Combined Hanan Shield Districts 6.
1977: Lions 45, Combined Hanan Shield Districts 6.
1983: Lions 26, Mid Canterbury 6.

Lancaster Park, Christchurch, 4 June.
Attendance: 45,000. Weather: sunny. Pitch: soft.

Lions 12 (O. Campbell 3 penalties, 1 drop goal).
All Blacks 16 (M. Shaw 1 try, A. Hewson 3 penalties,

1 drop goal).

Lions: H. MacNeill, T. Ringland, D. Irwin, R. Ackerman, R. Baird, O. Campbell, T. Holmes, I. Stephens, C. Fitzgerald (capt.), G. Price, M. Colclough, B. Norster, J. Squire, I. Paxton, P. Winterbottom. Sub, R. Laidlaw for Holmes.

All Blacks: A. Hewson, S. Wilson, S. Pokere, W. Taylor, B. Fraser, I. Dunn, D. Loveridge, J. Ashworth, A. Dalton (capt.), G. Knight, A. Hayden, G. Whetton, M. Shaw, M. Mexted, J. Hobbs.
Referee: F. Palmade (France).

CHAPTER 12

PURPLE PATCH

The West Coast of New Zealand's South Island is a world apart. Separated by the Southern Alps, which are snow-capped for most of the year, West Coasters have a different outlook on life from inhabitants of populous cities such as Auckland, Christchurch and Wellington — even, indeed, from those living in smaller towns elsewhere in the country.

Their rugby players are drawn from a wide hinterland with a total population of just 20,000; they have built a reputation for themselves as men of great effort, but against touring teams they have had little success. In their previous six games against the Lions (when they combined with Buller), they suffered crushing defeats. But they do not really mind being beaten. In a way, they see a good display by touring sides as a reward for the warm hospitality of their friendly inhabitants.

WEST COAST

The sunshine followed the Lions to the West Coast. The setting at Rugby Park, Greymouth was perfect, and although the Lions proceeded to make characteristic errors, they were a class apart from their opponents. The home spectators were more than happy with the seven tries they produced and especially with the one which their side scored as the Lions roared to a sound 52-16 victory.

The Lions side that day contained no Irishmen — for the first time on the tour — and the convincing manner in which they won was mainly due to the brilliant running of English winger John Carleton and the kicking abilities of fellow-countryman Dusty Hare.

Carleton was back to his best form, having missed the first test and he finished off a very polished performance with four tries. Hare, meanwhile, won the admiration of the crowd with almost perfect kicking. He contributed 24 points with four penalties and six conversions, and in fact only missed two kicks all afternoon.

The Scotsmen did the rest of the damage, with Roy Laidlaw captaining the side and scoring a try, and John Rutherford and John Beattie getting one each. If the game was not as memorable as it could have been, Laidlaw, the most personable of people, was delighted to have led the side. I recall speaking with him after the game when he asked, "Was it a record?" "No," I said, "the 1959 Lions scored 58 against them." "Pity," said Laidlaw, "but I was happy to have been chosen as captain for the day anyway."

The Lions might well have broken that 1959 record, for they totally dominated this game. The pack to a man towered over the opposition. I remember thinking early in the game that the West Coast forwards, in comparison, looked like a set of light-weight prop forwards with players such as Steve Boyle, Steve Bainbridge, Nick Jeavons and John Beattie appearing as giants alongside them.

I do not intend to detract from the Lions' performance, for any side that scores seven tries must have performed well. They certainly did. But the total could have been a great deal more had there been more cohesion in midfield. The match was another example of how badly Clive Woodward had lost his form. A player of enormous potential, Woodward just failed to regain the form that had made him one of the great centres a few seasons ago. Against such weak opposition, one hoped that he would come good, but despite fleeting moments of brilliance, he did not.

The result was that some movements which might well have led to an avalanche of tries did not materialise and but for the hard running and precise finishing of Carleton, the Lions might well have struggled against a gallant but totally outplayed West Coast side.

The home team actually took the lead after nine minutes when full-back Wayne Gugich kicked a penalty, but Rutherford got the first Lions' try two minutes later. Hare converted and then kicked two penalties before Gugich got one back for the West Coast. And soon the Lions were leading by a frail six points with only five minutes of the first half remaining. Luckily for them their pressure paid off and by half-time they had settled with a 15-point lead. Carleton got the first of his tries, Hare converted and then kicked two further penalties after Gugich had got his third.

Then the Lions stamped their full authority on the game with Laidlaw nipping over for a try which Hare converted; and while Gugich struck another penalty, Carleton was in again after 15 minutes, Hare converting that as well as a John Beattie try later. Once again Carleton struck and Hare converted and if West Coast had their moment of joy with a Kevin Ford try, the Lions finished the scoring with another Carleton try.

SOUTHLAND

Over the years Southland have met touring teams and their record has been a highly successful one. They have beaten Australia eight times, France once, Fiji a couple of times and the Lions twice also.

Little wonder, then, that the selectors should choose a strong side to meet them. Southlanders were relishing the thought of a third victory over the Lions, having won in 1950 by 11-0 and in 1966 by 14-8. The Lions, apart from their game in 1971 when they fashioned a 25-3 win, have always found Southland a tough proposition.

McBride and Telfer knew exactly what to expect, for they had both seen action here together in 1966, and they met the challenge head-on by naming a very strong side.

Southland, although only a second division side which

had failed narrowly the previous season to win promotion, were expected to provide the Lions with problems and one had no doubt about this in the opening few minutes of the game. But this was one which the Lions were not about to let away and the history books will show that by the end they had handed out a severe thrashing to the home side, inflicting upon them their biggest ever defeat by a touring team.

Not alone did Southland concede over 40 points for the first time, but they gave the tourists their third highest score on the tour up to then, and their biggest victory margin.

Southland simply crumbled after a magnificent effort at the start and the Lions cruised away effortlessly to score six tries, bettered only by the seven they got against West Coast.

The Irish played a big part in their success. Michael Kiernan and David Irwin were in partnership for the second time on tour and each scored a try while playing a part in some of the others. Trevor Ringland made one for Jim Calder and scored another, while star débutant, the uncapped English scrum-half, Nigel Melville, scored two.

Ciaran Fitzgerald was a key figure in the victory, for he was always in the thick of the action, tidying up the line-outs and scurrying around in the most business-like fashion imaginable. And as for John O'Driscoll, well, he was just superb. Showing no signs of discomfort from the rib injury which had kept him out of action for three weeks, O'Driscoll provided the Lions with a major trump card by putting Iain Paxton and Jim Calder totally in control at the back of the line-out.

The pack provided enough possession for the game to be won many times over. There was some criticism of the Lions' backline. This was partly justified, for at times in the first half they did not always use the ball to the greatest advantage. John Rutherford, for a start, was taking the ball standing from the lightning-fast Melville; David Irwin kicked once or twice when running might have been more

172

rewarding; and Michael Kiernan missed one bad tackle. But these were momentary lapses and the fact is that this back-line looked exciting for much of the game. A fitting tribute is that the backs provided five of the six tries.

Rutherford, in a gifted and skilful way, made a mockery of the Southland defence when he decided to run, Irwin breezed through for a great first half-try, and Kiernan's and Ringland's powerful running confined the latter stages of the match. All these movements were the topics of conversation after the final whistle.

The first four minutes of the game were not happy ones for the Lions as Southland threw everything into attack. But their failure to score then — and they came close when former All Black Brian McKechnie missed a penalty goal — meant that their challenge quickly evaporated.

Ten minutes after the start, Dusty Hare kicked a penalty and added another in 13 minutes. Irwin's strength was emphasised when he broke a tackle to get in for a try after 18 minutes and again Hare converted. McKechnie did kick a penalty after 24 minutes but the strength of the Lions was bound to tell and after 31 minutes they went further ahead. Fitzgerald took a strike against the head near the Southland line and Rutherford broke on the blind before sending the supporting Melville in. Gwyn Evans, who shortly before had replaced the injured Hare, converted, and then in injury time John Rutherford dropped a goal.

The romp, apart from a brief respite from Southland, continued in the second half and in 14 minutes a spectacular run infield by Ringland set up a try for Calder at the posts and Evans converted. Ten minutes from the end, a brilliant break by Robert Norster and Iain Paxton set Melville up for his second try, and two minutes later, Kiernan was there in support of Paxton and he cut through the defence to score his second try of the tour.

Evans converted that but failed to add the points to the last try, scored by Ringland after Rutherford, Calder, Irwin and Kiernan had all been involved in a movement which started 40 yards out. The rout was complete.

Left or right, inside or outside: that was the problem facing Irishmen David Irwin and Michael Kiernan, the midfield duo named for the match against Wairarapa-Bush, the first division outfit tipped to stretch the Lions in their last match before the second test.

In New Zealand a first centre is referred to as second five eighth and a second centre simply as centre. To put it simply, they stick to their positions on the field. And when the Lions' party left London, coach Telfer informed the players he wanted them to play that way too, but the strategy, while at times threatening to work, posed some problems and discomfort for the players.

Kiernan told me early in the tour that although he would be happy to play anywhere in a Lions jersey, particularly in a test, he found it difficult to settle as an outside-centre. The others, Irwin, Robert Ackerman and Clive Woodward all felt the same. Having gone through two seasons of international rugby for Ireland, partnering both Paul Dean and then his fellow Lion, David Irwin, he was used to alternating between the two — in other words, playing left and right. Neither he nor Irwin felt they had settled into the new routine, so on the eve of the match against Wairarapa-Bush, a match they were expected to win anyway, they approached Telfer and requested a reversion to the old way. Telfer, a man not unknown to take advice from the players with whom he had built up a good relationship, acceded.

The result was a more potent, fluent backline, which absolutely devastated a bemused Wairarapa-Bush side. The Lions ran in for nine tries, their biggest total of the tour and seven of them came from the backs.

In a subsequent interview with me, on the morning when he learned of his selection for the second test in Wellington, Kiernan referred to the fact that each of the wingers scored two tries, the full-back scored two also and that David Irwin had added one too. "I don't think I was more relaxed," said Kiernan, "It was just like old times where you knew what your partner was going to do. And I think we were completely confident in the way we played."

Masterton is situated about 60 miles the other side of the mountains. As in almost every place in New Zealand, the players treat their rugby pretty seriously, particularly in the last year or so, after they won promotion from the second division. Although they had never, in six previous games, beaten the Lions, they anticipated putting up a good show.

They wanted a good result, if not for themselves, then for Bill Rowlands, their veteran prop-forward who, amazingly, had played against the Lions in 1966, 1971 and 1977. The home crowd afforded Rowlands, who, although not captain, led his side onto the pitch, rapturous applause before the start of the game.

Although they were fired with determination, Wairarapa-Bush were on a loser this time, for they met a Lions' side equally determined. This was a chance for the side to have a useful workout for the test, for the established players to cement their positions and for those on the fringes to mount a challenge. The end-product was a rip-roaring match, with the Lions doing most of the roaring.

There were moments in the first half when, holding a nine-point lead, they had to pool all their resources to reject a mighty Wairarapa-Bush assault. And they needed a goal-kicker for they missed four scoreable penalties, all at a time when the game was still very much alive.

But the Lions, for whom Baird had scored a try and Campbell had converted while also kicking a penalty, came back to lead 15-0 at the interval, with John Carleton getting a try just before the break, one also converted by Campbell.

And then, having conceded a try to Kevin Carter within a minute of the resumption, the Lions cut loose. Gwyn Evans got in for a try which Campbell converted, Campbell kicked a penalty and then Irwin got in for a beautiful try to which Campbell again added the points.

Midway through the half, Baird got in for his second try,

taking the scoring pass from Kiernan; and if Wairarapa-Bush got their second try from Chris Kapene, which Carter converted, the Lions replied again when Evans scored and Campbell converted.

The strength of the Lions' scrum was emphasised when John Beattie got in for two tries after set pieces near the home line. Campbell converted the second of them, Michael Kiernan dropped a goal and then the Irishman sent Carleton away on a 60-yard run for another try in the corner.

THE SECOND TEST

Ollie Campbell clasped his hand to his head in the foyer of the team hotel in Wellington after the Lions had decisively lost the second test and thought for a moment. "No, I cannot remember the last time I did not have a kick at goal in any match," he said.

Incredible though it may seem, Campbell, the ace goal-kicker, the man who had won the respect of New Zealand rugby followers, the man whom they feared the most in this series, got no chance at all as the All Blacks thundered their way to a classical victory which put them 2-0 up in the series.

There were, in all, three penalties given in the second half of this game. One of them fell to the Lions but it was so deep inside their own half as not to afford Campbell any opportunity of kicking a goal. The out-half was quite sad, and admitted that the Lions had a huge amount of improving to do if they were to entertain hopes of even sharing the series. The match was, in my view, spoiled by a huge wind on a bitterly cold day, but Campbell was quick to point out that "wind by itself never won any match. It is how it is used and how a team adapts to the problems it brings. We were never going to win that game," he stressed.

New Zealand second row star Andy Hayden summed it up by saying the match boiled down to two simple things: The All Blacks wanted to win, the Lions had to win. He said: "One must feel sorry now for the Lions who have to fight desperately for a drawn series. If we play better their chances seem dismal, but I think they can take consolation from the fact that we were close to our maximum, especially up front."

A team talk at half-time by captain Andy Dalton seems to have worked wonders, for then the All Blacks held a mere 9-0 lead, won while they enjoyed the benefit of the gale. Dalton told his men that the nine points might not be enough but that if they won this one it would be one of the great All Black victories.

When you have an All Black pack playing for pride, and a half-back of the quality of Dave Loveridge in superlative form, you have a test match victory at hand.

The pack were absolutely magnificent, but Loveridge stole the show. Afterwards, coach Bryce Rope described it as his test: "Dave's performance was worthy to be put alongside the best of anyone in test match history. I have rarely seen anything like it."

Willie John McBride joined in the praise: "The All Blacks were superb in the second half, and Loveridge was the real star." McBride added that they had been beaten in every facet of forward play. Coach Jim Telfer said that the scrummaging was the key factor, the All Blacks having improved out of all proportion in that area since Christchurch. He continued: "Their play on the loose ball was always very effective and at times brilliant. In contrast, the ball we got was very scrappy and difficult to get away." Captain Ciaran Fitzgerald pointed to the All Blacks' sharpness, particularly in the second half. "They played extremely well," he added.

What happened the scrummaging was something which must have worried any Lions' supporters, but I believe, and on sound advice too, that it had something to do with injuries to Iain Paxton, which necessitated his being replaced by John Beattie, and to second row Robert Norster.

In the hotel later that evening I spoke to Norster, who was clearly in pain after receiving a back injury. He informed me that his back had begun to stiffen a few days before the match but he thought it would be all right; in fact, it got progressively worse as the game went on. Norster was in the difficult situation of having to stay on the field. He told me: "Iain had already been replaced and there was no second row forward on the bench. I wanted to stay on, and I felt I had to even though the pain was immense. And I know that I was the one weak link in the scrums."

I recall remarking to a colleague in the press box only minutes into the second half how strong the Lions scrum was. Later on things began to go wrong, inexplicably, it seemed at the time. I believe Norster's injury must have had something to do with it.

The loss of any test is a major disappointment for the players concerned, even more so when one realises that a series victory is out of reach. The evening's activities were rather muted as the team reflected on the afternoon's happenings.

Yet, despite the grim faces, some still managed a smile. Norster told me the most annoying thing was that the players felt they could beat the New Zealanders: "If only we can all put it together on the day of a test, which we have not done. But we still have a belief in ourselves."

And Irishman David Irwin, reflecting not alone on the loss of the match, but also on the loss of a Lions' dinner jacket to a mean thief in Wellington the day before, said: "Damn it, we'll just have to put up with a draw!" From those and other remarks, it was clear that there was still some fight left in the Lions. But would that be enough?

The Lions had their moments in the game and indeed the second-half might have been a different affair if referee Francis Palmade, usually one to allow advantage, had not been so hasty in whistling up an All Black infringement before half time. The tourists trailed by those nine points but home full-back Allan Hewson failed to catch a high kick on his line. The inevitable scurry for possession followed and Fitzgerald picked up to crash over in the corner for a perfectly legitimate try. The sad thing was that referee Palmade whistled for the knock on by Hewson.

To mention that, I suppose, is pure conjecture, for the All Blacks were so far ahead in thought that they might well have doubled their eventual total. They too had numerous chances and if their claims for a second half-try by Steve Pokere were of dubious intent and waved away by the Frenchman, it was nevertheless a lucky escape for the Lions.

In any case Loveridge did enough to destroy their hopes of squaring the series with a smashing try in the sixteenth minute of the first half, breaking from a ruck near the line and selling a dummy before sneaking in on the blind side for the try which Hewson converted. The full-back kicked a thirty-first minute penalty and that ended the scoring.

EIGHTH MATCH: WEST COAST
Rugby Park, Greymouth, 8 June.
Attendance: 5,200. Weather: sunny. Pitch: firm.

Lions 52 (J. Carleton 4 tries, J. Rutherford, R. Laidlaw, J. Beattie 1 try each, D. Hare 6 conversions, 4 penalties). *West Coast* 16 (W. Gugich 4 penalties, K. Ford 1 try).

Lions: D. Hare, J. Carleton, C. Woodward, R. Ackerman, G. Evans, J. Rutherford, R. Laidlaw (capt.), S. Jones, C. Deans, I. Milne, S. Boyle, S. Bainbridge, N. Jeavons, J. Beattie, J. Calder.

West Coast: W. Gugich, D. King, G. Power, D. Lynch, M. McIntosh, G. Cook, K. Ford, J. Walton, G. Patterson, P. Davidson, T. Price, T. Forsyth, A. Bruhn, G. McGurk, B. Hopkins (capt.).
Referee: T. Gresson (South Canterbury).

Lions Record against West Coast and District Sides
1930: Lions 34, West Coast/Buller 11.
1950: Lions 32, West Coast/Buller 3.

1959: Lions 58, West Coast/Buller 3.
1966: Lions 25, West Coast/Buller 6.
1971: Lions 39, West Coast/Buller 6.
1977: Lions 45, West Coast/Buller 0.
1983: Lions 52, West Coast 16.

NINTH MATCH: SOUTHLAND
Rugby Park, Invircargill, 11 June.
Attendance: 19,000. Weather: sunny and warm.
Pitch: firm.

Lions 41 (N. Melville 2 tries, D. Irwin, M. Kiernan, T. Ringland, J. Calder 1 try each, D. Hare 2 penalties and 1 conversion. G. Evans 3 conversions, J. Rutherford 1 drop goal).
Southland 3 (B. McKechnie 1 penalty).

Lions: D. Hare, J. Carleton, D. Irwin, M. Kiernan, T. Ringland, J. Rutherford, N. Melville, I. Stephens, C. Fitzgerald (capt.), G. Price, M. Colclough, R. Norster, J. O'Driscoll, I. Paxton, J. Calder. Reserves: G. Evans for Hare, S. Jones for Stephens.

Southland: B. McKenzie, J. Cormack, S. Pokere, R. Laidlaw, B. Dickinson, B. McKechnie, C. Hiini, P. Cosgrove, L. Chisholm, D. Murcott, F. Darmody, A. Byrne, P. Henderson, B. Robertson, L. Ruttledge.
Referee: B. Francis (Wairarapa-Bush).

Lions Record against Southland
1930: Lions 9, Southland 3.
1950: Lions 11, Southland 0.
1959: Lions 11, Southland 6.
1966: Lions 14, Southland 8.
1971: Lions 25, Southland 3.
1977: Lions 20, Southland 12.
1983: Lions 41, Southland 3.

TENTH MATCH: WAIRARAPA-BUSH
Memorial Park, Masterton, 14 June.
Attendance: 12,000. Weather: fine. Pitch: firm.

Lions 57 (J. Carleton, R. Baird, G. Evans, J. Beattie 2 tries each, D. Irwin 1 try, O. Campbell 6 conversions, 2 penalties, M. Kiernan 1 drop goal).
Wairarapa-Bush 10 (K. Carter 1 try conversion, G. Kopene 1 try).

Lions: G. Evans, J. Carleton, D. Irwin, M. Kiernan, R. Baird, O. Campbell, R. Laidlaw, S. Jones, C. Deans, I. Milne, S. Bainbridge, S. Boyle, J. O'Driscoll, J. Beattie, P. Winter-bottom.

Wairarapa-Bush: N. Kjestrup, G. Karaitiana, K. Carter, C. Kaka, M. Cornford, P. Rutene, B. Anderson, B. Rowlands, G. McGlashan, C. Kapene, D. White, M. McCool, B. Harvey, C. Baker, T. Hullena.
Referee: K. Anderston (Otago).

Lions Record against Wairarapa-Bush
1930: Lions 19, Wairarapa-Bush 6.
1950: Lions 27, Wairarapa-Bush 13.
1959: Lions 37, Wairarapa-Bush 11.
1966: Lions 9, Wairarapa-Bush 6.
1971: Lions 27, Wairarapa-Bush 6.
1977: Lions 41, Wairarapa-Bush 13.
1983: Lions 57, Wairarapa-Bush 10.

ELEVENTH MATCH: THE SECOND TEST
Athletic Park, Wellington, 18 June
Attendance: 44,000. Weather: cold wind, sunny.
Pitch: firm.

Lions 0.
All Blacks 9 (D. Loveridge 1 try, A. Hewson 1 conversion and 1 penalty).

Lions: H. MacNeill, J. Carleton, D. Irwin, M. Kiernan, R. Baird, O. Campbell, R. Laidlaw, S. Jones, C. Fitzgerald (capt.), G. Price, M. Colclough, R. Norster, J. O'Driscoll, I. Paxton, P. Winterbottom. Reserve: J. Beattie for Paxton.

All Blacks: A. Hewson, S. Wilson, S. Pokere, W. Taylor, B. Fraser, W. Smith, D. Loveridge, J. Ashworth, A. Dalton (capt.), G. Knight, A. Hayden, G. Whetton, M. Shaw, M. Mexted, J. Hobbs.
Referee: F. Palmade.

CHAPTER 13

HOPE SPRINGS ETERNAL

The spirits of the Lions were dampened considerably as they headed for Waitangi in the Bay of Islands for a well-deserved three-day rest. There, despite one training session, the players were able to relax for the first time on tour. They had no mid-week fixture and so had time on their hands to soak up the sun, take traditional boat cruises, go deep sea fishing, snorkling, diving or try their hand at golf. Here they tried their best to put the events of the weekend behind them, and slowly but surely build up to the next test.

The Bay of Islands is one of the most idyllic spots in the country and even the press corps, many of whom had got used to filing two or more stories a day, found time to unwind.

Across the bay from Waitangi lies Russell, or Kororareka as it was previously known — New Zealand's first settlement. Today it is a mere village with just one hotel. But in the old days it was known as the "hell hole" of the Pacific, its narrow foreshore lined with makeshift buildings housing drinking parlours and brothels. Russell was the scene of wild revelry and the exploitation of maori girls and women for the pleasure of visiting seamen from whaling and sealing vessels. How times have changed . . .

In the still air of a warm peaceful day, I talked with Graham Price, the experienced Welsh prop-forward. "No, we have not given up hope", he said, getting back to rugby. "Despite all our problems, there is a lot of character in this side."

The following day, we were in Whangarei, an hour's drive to the South, and for everybody, it was back to work. Trevor Ringland, who had just finished a training session, remarked: "It's like coming from the old world into the new." Yes, back to work indeed. And as North Auckland were to prove, that work was cut out for the Lions . . . in more ways than one.

Already in that training stint on the Thursday before the game, the team had suffered a cruel blow when Ian Stephens, who had been injured in the Southland match, collapsed with a recurrence of his knee ligament troubles, and that evening he was ruled out of the tour.

But on match day they were to suffer another blow — on the double. Nigel Melville, who had looked a classy player on his début against Southland, was the object of a short arm tackle from North Auckland flanker Ian Phillips which was to end his interest in the game; minutes later, Jeff Squire, the man on whom most were pinning their hopes for a Lions' victory in the third test, crashed to the ground in a bid to tackle scrum-half Chris Hull, damaging again the shoulder ligaments which he thought had healed. That injury put an end to his participation in the tour.

The double blow could have had serious consequences against a side such as North Auckland, who, although out of their depth when destroyed 44-0 by Queensland only a couple of weeks before, were to provide the Lions with a game they would not forget easily.

Sitting next to me in the stand was Sid Going, a man revered in New Zealand rugby, particularly in North Auckland. Going was one of the greatest scrum-halves the world has ever known and the esteem in which he is held throughout the country is highlighted by an article in the match programme in which the author pointed out some pertinent points about his career.

"Super Sid" often caused panic in opposing sides even before they took the field simply because they knew he was there. It is true that he put hundreds, sometimes thousands of dollars onto normal gates; that he caused a test match crowd in Wellington to cheer and stamp when, as a reserve, he was called on the field; that he brought comment from All Black colleague Ian Kirkpatrick that the selectors, committed to naming a side without him, left Sid out of the All Black trials because they were afraid he would make them look silly; and that he continued to receive fan mail of the quantity usually reserved for film stars, even in the twilight of his career.

Going is a quiet man. A bishop in the Mormon Faith, he was awarded the MBE for his service to rugby. But when it comes to being a spectator, he was not so quiet but seemed delighted that his province had done so well.

Yet his comments about the Lions were gracious. He admitted that they had not been particularly impressive in victory, yet he commented: "They may not have played well, but do not write them off. This side has had more than its share of criticism, but I think they are a good team. It is much easier for a provincial team to peak for a match of this nature than it would be for the Lions, who I feel will come good before the end of the tour."

The Lions were forced, however, to rely on the boot of Campbell to get them out of this one. They led 15-3 with only ten minutes of the second half gone, and should have coasted away. Instead, they allowed North Auckland, a spirited and clever running side back into it and when the home team got to within three points, I felt it was all over. But enter Ollie, who kicked two penalty goals, the last a minute from the end, and that was that.

North Auckland took the lead midway through the first half with a Geoff Valli penalty and it took the Lions a long time to get back into it, with Campbell finally dropping a goal in injury time. Their best spell came after the re-start when Robert Ackerman finished off an orthodox blind side movement with a blistering run. Campbell converted and then he played a major role in a try by Jim Calder seven minutes later, before also converting.

Valli started a home revival with a penalty and he added the points after Ian Phillips crashed over for a try at the posts. But Campbell came to the rescue with penalties in the thirty-first and fortieth minutes which would see the Lions through.

The Lions had won, but the casualties suffered were to hurt them hard. No doubt about it, the tackle on Melville was illegal, but if McBride had a right to complain after the match, then he should surely have commented earlier on an incident involving Steve Bainbridge and Phillips when the North Auckland match was butted in the face. That was one of the most silly acts I had seen on tour and had it been seen by the referee it would surely have been punished with a sending off.

CANTERBURY

Ranfurly Shield holders, Canterbury, were next on the list, and they were there for the pickings despite their reputation and despite their talent and determination. The Lions lost 20-22 and if ever a match was thrown away, this was it. But the selectors more than the players must take the blame, for they allowed a side to take the pitch without an established goal-kicker.

They banked on Hugo MacNeill to do the job — a man who has kicked a few long range goals for Ireland. They put tremendous pressure on a player fighting to retain his test place and paid the price.

The selectors were correct to rest Ollie Campbell and probably correct too in making MacNeill fight for his test position, for Gwyn Evans had started to mount a strong challenge. But what they surely should have done, and this is not merely said in hindsight, was to play Evans on the wing instead of Roger Baird, who had proved that he was the number one winger in the party before that. He did not have to prove it again. Evans, with the number of chances provided for the Lions, would surely have kicked them to victory.

MacNeill missed four penalties in the first half, three of them relatively easy, and then under severe pressure sent a last minute conversion attempt skidding across the face of the posts and so, a draw, which in the circumstances would have been a good result for the Lions, went a-begging.

This is not an indictment on MacNeill, for quite simply it was grossly unfair to put him in the position where he would not only be playing for his test place, but also be chief goal-kicker as well. The Lions then slumped to their fourth defeat of the tour and their second in provincial matches. But if the disappointment was enormous, they can look back and recall that this had all the ingredients of a classic.

It was heady stuff indeed with the Lions trailing at the interval and then coming back in spectacular fashion to take the lead, then to lose it again before striking in injury time with a try which should, had either Campbell, Hare or Evans been there, have assured them a share of the spoils.

From Canterbury's point of view it was a momentous victory, their third over the Lions in seven matches, and for their full-back Robbie Deans, who had been living in the shadow of Allan Hewson, it was a marvellous afternoon. Deans had been put forward by the local fans as number one full-back for quite some time, but Hewson was the main full-back to win the test place. But on this display, one of perfection, Deans proved a point and almost single-handedly destroyed the Lions, getting a lot of help from a marvellous number eight, Dale Atkins.

Atkins was, after Deans, the star performer and the Lions did not have a forward to match him as he drove ahead, smashing the touring players out of his way with spectacular success.

Of course the Lions performed well themselves at times, and indeed they proved themselves better equipped at try-scoring, getting three to Canterbury's two. But in the end that was not enough, for they did not have a goal kicker of Deans' quality and while MacNeill was sending his pots wide, Deans was slotting his between the posts.

At half-time it read: Deans 12, Lions 3. Deans kicked a penalty after two minutes, scored a try and converted it in 26 minutes and then added another penalty before the break, with the Lions' only score, despite their having done quite well in the first half, coming from a long range MacNeill penalty after 21 minutes.

Again the period immediately after the interval was a fruitful one for the Lions, with John Rutherford getting a drop goal after eight minutes, Roger Baird a try two minutes later and then Iain Paxton another in 16 minutes, one which MacNeill converted.

That should have been enough to see them through, for they were then firmly on top. But Canterbury reacted positively by coming back to earn themselves a penalty goal which Deans kicked; the brilliant Atkins charged over for a try and then Deans pounced again. The game was almost over when the Lions launched one final assault and David Irwin got in for a try but, of course, the conversion was beyond MacNeill.

THE THIRD TEST

Two days before the last test between the Lions and South Africa in 1980, the tour from an injury point of view, was akin to that of New Zealand, when English scrum-half Steve Smith arrived as a replacement. As John Robbie and himself were the only fit men in that position, Smith was called upon to sit on the bench as a replacement. He never became a Lion and when he returned home his first job was to have the Lions badge removed from his blazer.

As the injury list was rapidly growing, Smith, along with Irishmen McLoughlin and Lenihan, arrived in Christchurch on the Tuesday before the test and broke his South African record by immediately togging off as a replacement. He found himself in a similar situation to the 1980 team for the third New Zealand test.

The build-up, from the Lions' point of view, was not too impressive. They had gone down 2-0 in the series, had been troubled by North Auckland and lost to Canterbury. The team and, with the smear campaign continuing, captain Fitzgerald must have been going through a crisis of confidence, even if outwardly the party seemed to be holding up well. I paid regular visits to the team hotel to maintain contact, and the mood, on the surface, seemed no different from that prevailing when they were eagerly awaiting their second clash with the All Blacks.

Hugo MacNeill was one of three Irishmen to lose his test place. He may have had reason to be sore with the selectors, but he was not: "I think in a situation like this, one has to ask oneself have I been playing as well as I can and if the answer is no then there are no real grounds for complaint. I think I did well defensively, but I have not always had the opportunity to join the line and even when I did, it did not always work out for me."

On the subject of team morale, MacNeill was as forthright as the rest. "There is no doubt that our confidence has been shaken a little but I don't believe our heads are bowed. We know what the party is capable of. We know the All Blacks are beatable. It's just a question of getting everything right on the day."

Dave Irwin and John O'Driscoll were two others to lose out. Irwin had had a most satisfactory tour but the lack of penetration by the backline as a whole had been a constant source of worry to the selectors and if Rutherford did not altogether set the world alight when tried in the centre against North Auckland, the men in charge had some backing for slotting him in there. A risk was taken in naming Jim Calder as one of the two flankers. Not because he had played badly on previous games, but because he was to partner Peter Winterbottom, thus giving the Lions two open-sided flankers — a departure from the norm which many disagreed with, although some were in favour of it because it indicated that the Lions were intent on an all-out attacking game.

Dunedin can be a cruel place in mid-winter, and it turned out such in more ways than one. On a tour which had

189

taken the players and press corps thousands of miles, the weather had been more than kind. But on arrival in a city which had its roots firmly entrenched in Scottish history, it was surprising to find that the conditions were somewhat similar to those one would expect in Edinburgh on a bad winter's day. But if Dunedin has many similarities with the Scottish capital, even Edinburgh could not throw up the same type of howling gales and driving incessant rain which left Carisbrook looking more like a pond than a rugby pitch.

The players — from both sides I hasten to add — trained during the preceding two days in appalling conditions. I don't think I have ever known worse. The Lions, in their training stint on the outskirts of the city, were saturated by the continuous deluge within seconds of taking to the pitch, while the All Blacks, further out and closer to the nearby mountainous region, shivered their way through a blizzard — some of them at any rate.

The backs, who for obvious reasons take longer to warm up and who can never be guaranteed staying warm, took the wise precaution of wearing special rubber vests provided for them by an underwater diving company and so satisfied were they with them that they decided they would also use them on match day. Word of that was picked up by the Lions' management, and they, too, sent for a consignment for their players.

Five of the backs, Gwyn Evans and Ollie Campbell excluded, wore them and after the game had ended, the odd men out both admitted readily that they regretted their decision. Evans told me it was not too bad during the first half, but that after the break he nearly "froze to death". Campbell added: "My feet were numb. I was never so cold in my life."

The All Blacks — Allan Hewson, Steve Pokere and Stu Wilson, at any rate — went even further by wearing gloves, while although not noticed, Bernie Fraser later said that he had covered his feet with plastic bags inside his stockings to keep the water out.

The pitch, holding water just under the surface, was a menace and in those circumstances it was amazing that the players managed to play quite a deal of good football in a match which may in years to come be dubbed "The vests and mittens test".

That the All Blacks won the game, thus securing the series, is now history and that Stu Wilson scored his 16th try to equal the All Black record previously held by Ian Kirkpatrick is also history. What the record books will not show is the gallant performance by the Lions in the face of a constant All Black barrage in the final quarter. That was where Wilson grabbed the all important try and when Hewson, maligned by many New Zealanders, showed his true class. He could do nothing wrong and when the Lions threatened to bash their way out of defence in that period, there was Hewson to send them reeling back again with a series of superb touchline kicks. He kept the pressure on them and was ultimately responsible for their defeat.

They say a team cannot win without the ball. That did not quite happen to the Lions, for in defence the forwards played magnificently and Steve Bainbridge, who played the game of his life in the line-outs, won quite a deal of possession close to his own line. It was however to no avail for both Roy Laidlaw and Campbell, who had begun promisingly enough, were unable to relieve the pressure. Laidlaw was unable to stabilise his service and Campbell unable to gain adequate ground from his kicks out of defence.

The Lions showed lots of flair and scored two tries to one for the All Blacks, but in that crucial period late in the match they were unable to match the New Zealanders for control.

It was that control which captain Fitzgerald referred to time and time again at the after-match dinner when he also took an opportunity to exact some revenge at some of the press corps who had attempted to undermine the morale of the party with attacks of various sorts. The mood of the players that night was surprisingly good as they cheerfully drank their fill and sang "We're On Tour" in the function room of the Southern Cross hotel. Fitzgerald received a standing ovation for his address in which he pointed out that only constructive criticism was welcome: "The Lions as individuals and as a team are on a world stage. The public have a right to know how we have performed, but a great deal of unjustified and untrue comments have been made about us. To those writers I say you are not doing the tour any good or you are not doing rugby football any good."

One of Fitzgerald's most consistent and vociferous critics, who seemed from the very beginning hell-bent on inducing a nervous breakdown, a man who was described to me by colleagues in indescribable terms, slunk from the room and was not present for the greater part of the captain's speech. He must have experienced telepathic signals. Or was it remorse? I doubt it. Such people are incapable of such feelings.

In any event Fitzgerald, as he had done on the pitch earlier that afternoon, stood up to be counted. He had thrown in four crooked balls (the main cause of the mud-slinging); Andy Dalton had similarly erred in the dreadful conditions with three.

Otherwise Fitzgerald had had a fine game. He had almost returned to his best after a couple of indifferent perform-ances. He was part of a pack stripped of star players such as Robert Norster, Ian Stephens and Jeff Squire, yet they all battled with a new-found zeal and even when the All Black power began to assert itself they never gave up in difficult uneasy defensive positions.

The Lions had a great start with a fine try by Roger Baird after nine minutes. Campbell lofted a high kick into the '22. The defence failed to clear, Bainbridge booted the ball on, Campbell also got a touch and Baird flew past the defence to dive on it as it headed towards the in-goal area.

They fell 6-4 behind by the interval though Hewson had kicked two penalties after both Laidlaw and Calder were caught offside from a scrum and a ruck respectively.

Yet they came back to score a try which, in the conditions, was superbly executed and which later earned the praise of All Black coach Bryce Rope. Calder and Paxton broke from a ruck near half-way, toeing the ball upfield. The Lions won a quick ruck and every back handled before the ball reached Baird. He cut inside and found Gwyn Evans who passed inside to Rutherford and the centre crashed over for the try which Campbell failed to convert.

The Lions were on top then and they held the initiative until almost into the third quarter. But then, after a series of raids, the All Blacks scored, Dave Loveridge sending Wilson away for a brilliant try with an inside pass. Hewson converted and with his side holding all the territorial gain, he finished them off with a penalty three minutes from the end.

TWELFTH MATCH: NORTH AUCKLAND
Okara Park, Whangarei, 25 June.
Attendance: 20,400. Weather: fine. Pitch: soft.

Lions 21 (R. Ackerman, J. Calder 1 try each, O. Campbell 2 penalty goals, 1 drop goal, 2 conversions).
North Auckland 12 (I. Phillips 1 try, G. Valdi 2 penalty goals, 1 conversion).

Lions: G. Evans, T. Ringland, J. Rutherford, M. Kiernan, R. Ackerman, O. Campbell, N. Melville, S. Jones, C. Fitzgerald (capt.), G. Price, S. Boyle, S. Bainbridge, N. Jeavons, J. Squire, J. Calder. Reserves: R. Laidlaw for Melville, J. Beattie for Squire.

North Auckland: G. Valli, K. Woodman, D. Haynes, C. Going, F. Woodman, I. Dunn, C. Hull, T. Perkinson, P. Sloane (capt.), L. Watene, J. Reid, A. Robinson, I. Phillips, N. Ruddell, B. Flavell.
Referee: G. Smith (Hawkes Bay).

Lions Record against North Auckland
1930: Lions 38, North Auckland 5.
1950: Lions 8, North Auckland 6.
1959: Lions 35, North Auckland 13.
1966: Lions 6, North Auckland 3.
1971: Lions 11, North Auckland 5.
1977: Lions 18, North Auckland 7.
1981: Lions 21, North Auckland 12.

THIRTEENTH MATCH: CANTERBURY
Lancaster Park, Christchurch, 28 June.
Attendance: 38,000. Weather: sunny. Pitch: softish.

Lions 20 (R. Baird, I. Paxton, D. Irwin 1 try each, H. MacNeill 1 penalty, 1 conversion, J. Rutherford 1 drop). *Canterbury* 22 (R. Deans 1 try, 4 penalty goals, 1 conversion, D. Atkins 1 try).

Lions: H. MacNeill, J. Carleton, D. Irwin, C. Woodward, R. Baird, J. Rutherford, R. Laidlaw, S. Jones, C. Deans, I. Milne, M. Colclough, S. Bainbridge, J. O'Driscoll, I. Paxton, P. Winterbottom.

Canterbury: R. Deans, G. Hooper, V. Simpson, W. Taylor, C. Creen, W. Smith, B. Deans, J. Ashworth, J. Willis, M. Davie, A. Anderson, T. Thorpe, D. Hayes (capt.), D. Atkins, J. Hobbs.
Referee: C. Dainty (Wellington).

Lions Record against Canterbury
1930: Canterbury 14, Lions 8.
1950: Lions 16, Canterbury 5.
1959: Canterbury 20, Lions 14.
1966: Lions 8, Canterbury 6.
1971: Lions 14, Canterbury 3.
1977: Lions 14, Canterbury 13.
1983: Canterbury 22, Lions 20.

FOURTEENTH MATCH: THE THIRD TEST
Carisbrook, Dunedin, 2 July.
Attendance: 30,000. Weather: rain.
Pitch: very wet, slippery.

Lions 8 (R. Baird and J. Rutherford 1 try each).
All Blacks 15 (S. Wilson 1 try, A. Hewson 3 penalties, 1 conversion).

Lions: G. Evans, J. Carleton, J. Rutherford, M. Kiernan, R. Baird, O. Campbell, R. Laidlaw, S. Jones, C. Fitzgerald (capt.), G. Price, M. Colclough, S. Bainbridge, J. Calder, I. Paxton, P. Winterbottom.

All Blacks: A. Hewson, S. Wilson, S. Pokere, W. Taylor, B. Fraser, W. Smith, D. Loveridge, J. Ashworth, A. Dalton (capt.), G. Knight, A. Hayden, G. Whetton, M. Shaw, M. Mexted, J. Hobbs.

CHAPTER 14

FITZGERALD'S REVENGE

After the bitterly cold conditions of Dunedin, it was pleasant for everyone to experience the mildness of Napier, the base for the fifteenth match of the tour against Hawkes Bay, a team not unknown to provide the Lions with tough challenges in the past.

Naturally the test defeat called for even more soul-searching but unlike the week in Bay of Islands and Whangarei, the Lions had a little less time to dwell on their problems.

Their stay in Napier was a happy one for although the hard work of training sessions and further plans had to be undertaken, the party still found time to enjoy themselves with visits to a local vineyard, to the Marineland of New Zealand with its performing dolphins, entertaining sea lions, leopard seals and fur seals and to the aquarium and oceanarium which housed an amazing variety of fish and reptiles in surroundings as close to their natural habitat as possible. It was there that the greatest "mud-slinger" of them all was aptly nicknamed "Piranha", after some of our vicious friends housed there.

HAWKES BAY

But back to rugby. The team to play Hawkes Bay included the three replacements flown out a week earlier, with Smith marking his début with the captaincy of the "Wednesday" side, and he, McLoughlin and Lenihan all performed well in the Lions' 25-19 win, even if the display of the team overall was not of vintage quality.

In fact the Lions' performance prompted former Wellington, Hawkes Bay and New Zealand representative John Dougan to describe the tourists as "poor". He said he was appalled at the number of errors they had made: "They won enough ball to do plenty with it, but the backs seemed obsessed with kicking the leather off it."

Willie John McBride was justified however in making some excuses: "The conditions were just the opposite to what they were in Dunedin. The ground made it hard for the players to control the bouncing ball, but having said that, I felt we put pressure on ourselves at times. But we settled down well in the second half and did very well in the last quarter."

Once again the side's plans were disrupted by injury. This time it was the turn of John Beattie, who limped from the field with a groin injury after 30 minutes and when it became clear after the game that he would be unable to play again, Welsh captain Eddie Butler was sent for as a replacement. That injury was indicative of the problems which the Lions have had to face on the tour.

It was a traditional performance from Hawkes Bay, who although never having beaten the Lions in previous encounters, had sometimes come mighty close — in 1977, for example, when the tourists escaped with a 13-11 win as Hawkes Bay missed seven shots at goal.

And it was a game that they might have won, had they not lost control up front in the last 30 minutes. They actually led 19-13 at the interval and although the Lions came back to equality immediately after the break, two missed penalty goals by Laurie Holmes might well have proved all-important.

But despite their rousing performance and their great ability to score tries — one of them undoubtedly the best we had seen on tour — the Lions deserved their win — just about.

They survived a hair-raising start and buckled down to

their task of taming "The Hawkeyes", as the home side are known in New Zealand.

Lenihan and McLoughlin both had marvellous second halves, with the Corkman mopping up the line-outs and McLoughlin scrummaging strongly on the loose side whilst contributing greatly to the Lions' powerful forward bursts.

Hawkes Bay were in front after just four minutes when Peter Dailey blocked down an attempted kick and he sent centre Nicky Allen racing away for a sensational try which Holmes converted.

Refereeing decisions have been mentioned elsewhere in this book, but I cannot think of any more stupid than one from Tom Doocey when the Lions were on the verge of scoring after seven minutes. The Hawkes Bay defence was offside but just as John Beattie was ready to pounce for the try, Doocey instead awarded a penalty which Dusty Hare then promptly missed from 25 yards. Yet they were rewarded five minutes later when David Irwin charged down a kick, gathered, found Hare and then Ringland, with the winger sending Colin Deans in for a try.

Iain Paxton grabbed the lead for the Lions only minutes after replacing Beattie when he got the touch after a five yard scrum, and Hare converted, but Holmes scored the try of the game just then when he came in at the speed of sound to take a flick pass from Allen and cut through for a try at the posts which he converted himself.

Hare kicked a penalty on a day when little went right for him — and that included a dislocated shoulder later on — but Neil Porter got another try for the home side to give them a six-point cushion at the break.

Rutherford, however, created a try for David Irwin two minutes after the resumption of play and although the centre crossed in the corner he cut back towards the posts to give Hare an easy shot at goal.

Holmes missed out with the penalty chances after that, and from then on it was the Lions all the way. Hare missed a penalty, Rutherford missed two drops at goals, Hugo MacNeill, a substitute for Hare, another, and Woodward a penalty, while they were denied tries on three occasions by stout defensive work. But the pressure had to pay off and they finally sealed the win to restore some sort of confidence in the side with a drop goal by Rutherford and a penalty by Woodward.

COUNTIES

"That's your only one," said All Black captain Andy Dalton as he left the field after Fitzgerald had led the Lions to a win over Counties. Dalton, who had been in such inspired form in the three tests, cannot be blamed for his side's defeat for he scored two tries. But even that contribution was not enough to save the game for Ollie Campbell was in magnificent kicking form and he shot the Lions to a memorable 25-16 win.

Both of Dalton's tries were scored in the corner as he came up to support his backline. At the press conference later he was asked when was the last time he had scored two tries. "I'd have to think hard as to when I last scored one try," he replied. Discussing the possibilities of New Zealand winning the fourth test, he thought for a moment, smiled, and said "it depends whether I'm allowed to play on the wing."

Dalton is equally at home in rugby and speech-making, but even he dismissed lightly his two try contributions. "It was nothing compared with Ollie's performance," he said.

Campbell may not have attacked with the same type of flair as he had done earlier in the tour, but his tackling was superb and his goal-kicking even better. He kicked five penalty goals and had two successful drops. His 21-point contribution brought his tour total to 97 and he set a new personal record with the longest goal-kick of his career, one struck from 59 metres. Aided by a strong tailwind, with Michael Kiernan steadying it for him, the ball cleared the crossbar by six feet and landed 15 yards behind the goal-line.

The Lions were none too happy with the performance

of referee Keith Lawrence (Bay of Plenty) who had also handled their first game against Wanganui. Dalton had no complaints: "I'm surprised. I think he kept control of things and I think the game flowed reasonably well. Christ, didn't they get enough shots at goal!" he grinned.

McBride had a point though, for if Lawrence did in fairness try to let the game run, he allowed Counties on more than one occasion to develop moves when the laws of the game had been broken. One particular movement allowed contained six infringements.

And what the Lions were reiterating of course is that they were not allowed to scrummage. Counties refused to pack down until they were forced to and three times in the game a scrummage was collapsed, with the Lions being penalised twice, when to bring it down would not have been to their advantage.

Fitzgerald said the Lions had again been forced to conform to a referee's interpretations. "We should not have to do that," he said.

The game and refereeing attitudes were not the only post-match talking points, for three of the Lions reserves were involved in a brawl with drunken spectators as they went for a training stint.

One of the New Zealand tabloids alleged that in this incident the players had been in the wrong. In fact it was the other way around. Gerry McLoughlin, Colin Deans and Eddie Butler, who had only that morning arrived in New Zealand were jogging on the pitch after the match when a spectator ran after McLoughlin and tripped him from behind. McLoughlin got up and chased his assailant, who escaped into the body of the stadium. As the players resumed their run, another man, showing obvious signs of drunkenness rushed at Deans, struck him and knocked him to the ground for no reason whatever. The assailant was struck by the other two players and kicked by Butler. While I am absolutely not an advocate of violence, the players had every right to protect their colleague and themselves for at that stage more inebriated fans were closing in for the kill.

The players wisely withdrew as the inebriated attackers were escorted away by security men and officials. It amazed me to see someone then trying to turn the incident into one of major proportions and it was even more incredible to discover that the same scribe did not even see the incident. He had received his information at second hand and twisted it to suit his own publication's requirements.

Nothing like that happened on the field of play, for it was a relatively clean match despite the tenseness. Counties were rated as highly as provinces such as Auckland and Canterbury who had both already taken the Lions "scalp". Yes, the men from "Cool Cat Country" had a lot to live up to, but although they played attractive, positive rugby, they were unable to exert the type of forward control necessary for victory.

Counties had some great moments in the loose, but after the break they failed, or were not allowed to assume any control. The Lions' pack played very well in that period, with Fitzgerald, Peter Winterbottom, John O'Driscoll, Steve Bainbridge and Donal Lenihan — who gave a magnificent display of line-out jumping — all taking the game to Counties and when, after holding an 18-6 half time lead, they went 21-6 up immediately after the resumption, the writing was on the wall for Counties.

They did pull back six points but then the Lions got their only try and from then on there was no chance of a Counties victory. Their second try came a minute from the end, far too late to make any difference.

Campbell kicked penalties in the fourth, tenth, nineteenth, twenty-second and twenty-sixth minutes and then dropped a goal in the thirtieth. Thirteen minutes into the game, Dalton got his first try which Joe Harvey superbly converted from the touch-line and that brought them to 6-6, but, as is already documented, Campbell sent them reeling with his succession of successful kicks. He dropped the second goal in the first minute of the second half, and while Harvey got his two penalties in the fourth and tenth minutes of the half, Nick Jeavons, and Steve Smith combined to send John Carleton in for a crucial try in 25 minutes. They held a firm edge after that, although Dalton got in for his late and second try.

WAIKATO

"Mooloo", another of the ridiculous mascots thrown up by New Zealand provincial sides, must indeed have been holding her udder as she watched the Lions romp to an impressive 40-13 victory, their biggest ever, over the province of Waikato.

This is dairying country and such is its importance that it has been known for kick-off times to be brought forward so that farmer rugby fans can get home in time for milking. A funny city, Hamilton, where, incidentally, the match was held.

New Zealanders are noted for more than their intense interest in rugby. They are also into PR and advertising in a big way. Can you imagine a pig farmer in Ireland with a sign outside his/her entrance, proclaiming "Pigs Are Beautiful", or a discount store owner saying "Come in and meet Jack the Slasher"? An obvious insult to the police force.

Before the kick-off, "Mooloo" was "milked" hence the normal kick-off time, and the symbolic gesture obviously did not help the Waikato players, some of whom were obviously keen to get back to their farms.

The Lions produced some brilliant rugby in a game which will be remembered as belonging to Ollie Campbell. The Irishman was at his very best. It was not his kicking, an aspect of his game which was keenly admired in a country where bouquets are not easily dispensed. No, it was his late try which had the home crowd in raptures and even if it cost him his fitness for the last test, it was a moment which I will remember for ever.

Jackie Kyle was the obvious comparison, but my knowledge of the brilliant Northerner is, I am afraid, very limited — limited, in fact, to qualified hearsay and the odd film clip. Campbell's try was enough, however, to give me an idea of how good Kyle must have been. It was magic, and why, I asked myself, could not a try of that quality have been scored more often by the Lions.

Scrum-half Roy Laidlaw fumbled the ball as it came back from a scrum 30 yards out but recovered well to break on the blind and he found Campbell coming inside in support. The Irishman then set off on a searing run, dummying and side-stepping his way past several defenders to crash over the line for a marvellous try. I watched it later on video at least six times and the only regret is that I did not secure a copy. Enough said!

Campbell converted to bring his points tally to 24, making him — like Dusty Hare — a point short of the individual scoring record in one match in New Zealand, and the saddest aspect was that he limped off with a hamstring injury immediately, one that was to curtail and finally end his action in the tour during the final test.

"Mooloo" then was crushed completely. But the damage had been done long before then, for this, in fact, was one of the better Lions' performances on tour, particularly because it came against a side expected to give them a rough ride before the last test. Perhaps it might have been better if they had.

Waikato began with seemingly deliberate intent to put someone away, and Roger Baird was the first victim of an amazingly late tackle by Waikato flanker Miah Nelson, whose enthusiasm really did the home side little good.

He was caught offside in three minutes and Campbell kicked his 100th point of the tour and while Tim Purcell brought them level with a penalty after 15 minutes, the score was very much against the run of the play. The tourists, apart from the odd lapse, had done most of the attacking and, as one colleague put it, "Clive Woodward finally arrived on tour." Woodward certainly looked the part and so it was sad to see him depart from the scene shortly after half-time suffering from an injury after being blatantly kicked in the back by a Waikato player.

In any event they had sealed the issue by then, for Colin Deans had pounced to score a try in the twenty-eighth minute, with Campbell converting and, after the out-half had kicked a penalty from the half-way line, Woodward set up a try for David Irwin to give them a 19-3 lead.

Campbell kicked another penalty two minutes into the second half and while Arthur Stone got in for a brilliant Waikato try six minutes later, there was to be no comeback.

Instead, Roy Laidlaw nipped in for a try when Deans took a strike against the head and Campbell converted; Irwin, Trevor Ringland, Campbell and Peter Winterbottom helped set up a try for Iain Milne which Campbell converted, and then came the Irishman's memorable effort which he converted himself.

That came six minutes from the end and Irwin was unlucky not to score a second time afterwards before Bruce Smith finally breached the Lions' defence with Richard Adam converting.

THE FOURTH TEST

The test score was 3-0, but there was still a chance for the Lions to save face and return home with their heads held aloft, as they had done in South Africa in 1980. That was the feeling within the camp as the preparations began for the fourth and final test, to be played at Eden Park, Auckland.

But the injury bogey that had followed the team around New Zealand from the second game, ironically on that same ground — when John O'Driscoll received a rib injury which was to keep him out of contention for three weeks and also affect his later form — continued.

John Rutherford, although failing to impress too much in his first outing as a centre against North Auckland, did extremely well in the third test in that position and looked set in the Counties match to realise his full potential when he suffered a groin strain. He would certainly have been selected for the last international, but the injury kept him out of the running and that, in addition to a niggling hamstring strain to Ollie Campbell, made going into the match a double hammer blow, psychologically at any rate.

These injuries must be taken into account although on the evidence of the All Blacks' performance, it scarcely made any difference. Nothing, but nothing could have stopped the New Zealanders romping to a comprehensive victory that day.

In the circumstances, the biggest blow was the injury to Campbell. David Irwin, who came in for Rutherford had a superb defensive game, and being realistic, neither he, or any other back for that matter, got a chance to show their prowess in attack, such was the limited amount of possession they received. So it can be taken that Rutherford was hardly missed. Campbell however, the man so vital throughout to the Lions' cause, was a sorry sight.

His injury was certainly not cleared up and indeed midway through the first half he left the field to have the leg strapped. He kicked a penalty goal after that and remained on until early in the second half. He finally accepted that the damage had got the better of him when a defensive mix-up between himself and Gwyn Evans let the All Blacks in for their fourth try, a mistake which I believe would never have occurred if the Irishman, always so strong defensively, had been fully fit.

At that time, indeed at any time, Campbell would have made little difference to the game, and so to dwell on the point is probably folly. This time there was no stopping the All Blacks who played with the type of commitment that the Lions should have had.

The match not alone showed them to be a superb footballing side, but also a tactically aware group who were much too clever for the Lions. Writing in the New Zealand Sunday paper, the *Times,* second row Andy Hayden said on the following day: "We realised that to start well would throw doubt into the minds of the Lions' players."

And that is how the rot began, because in the first few minutes the All Blacks played "out of their skins", stretching the Lions defence left and right, left and right. They established control so early that by the first quarter one felt the match would never end. It was a question of how much they would lose by, rather than, could they win?

The end-product was a resounding victory for the All Blacks, a new record for them over the Lions and a new record for the tourists, only in their case one they will want to forget. New Zealand scored six tries to none, Stu Wilson shattered the country's try scoring record with a hat trick of tries, and their overall level of play was streets ahead of a touring side which, long before the end, had resigned themselves to their fate.

In an interview the following day, Maurice Colclough told New Zealand colleague Ian Gault: "The All Blacks display was so good we now know how Davy Crockett felt at the Alamo. It wasn't that all our tackling was bad, we just ran out of people to tackle the All Blacks."

That was a pertinent point, for the Lions spent much of the match in defence. This was the All Blacks at their very best, and while there are those who will say the Lions were bad, I could not see any side in the world coping with the kind of play produced by the New Zealanders on this occasion. Amazingly fired up for the occasion they ripped into the Lions straight from the kick-off and continued to completely dictate the trend of the game for all but a brief spell towards the end. By then they had not only consolidated their position but had ensured that the result would be the worst in the history of the Lions.

The problems began and ended up front where the All Blacks dominated the set pieces, winning the vast majority of the line-out possession save for some good work by Steve Bainbridge, and disrupting the Lions scrum on their own put-ins. Around the field, Ciaran Fitzgerald, Bainbridge, Peter Winterbottom and sometimes John O'Driscoll threatened, but in the face of wave after wave of All Black power, their efforts seemed like crumbs off a small table.

Going forward the New Zealanders were unstoppable with the back five of Andy Hayden, Gary Whetton, Mark

Shaw, Murray Mexted and Jack Hobbs an awe-inspiring force. The Lions simply had nothing to match them, either in strength or in spirit.

The backs in those circumstances were on a hiding to nothing yet some of them performed admirably. From a defensive point of view, Irwin can hardly have had a more distinguished game and in the face of constant pressure, John Carleton, Michael Kiernan and Gwyn Evans brought off some fine tackles. There was no real opportunity to show themselves in attack although Carleton had a couple of good runs.

It would be easy to look back and say that some of those men, and that includes reserve Hugo MacNeill, made mistakes which allowed the All Blacks in for tries, but this was pressure rugby at its best. The home side exerted that pressure up front and the cracks were bound to appear somewhere. In some respects it was only magnificent tackling at times which curtailed the score-line.

They could not, however, stop the All Blacks from racing in for six tries, the first of which went to Hobbs after Allan Hewson had kicked two penalty goals in the third and eleventh minutes, following bouts of pressure. Steve Pokere made it to the line after a brilliant run but Evans took him short and the Lions were awarded the scrum. The All Blacks wheeled it, Hobbs picked up and went in unopposed for a try which Hewson converted.

Campbell kicked his penalty shortly afterwards but they were never able to assume control and fell further behind when Wilson was sent away by Fraser for his seventeenth international try to break the record he had shared with Ian Kirkpatrick.

He got in again a minute after the resumption and then Hewson took advantage of the mix-up between Evans and Campbell to race away for a try and convert himself. Andy Hayden charged in near the posts for the fifth try which Hewson converted midway through the half and in 29 minutes an intended flip pass by substitute MacNeill to Robert Ackerman, who only minutes before had replaced the injured Roger Baird, went astray and Wilson seized on the error to grab his third try, with Hewson again converting.

That was the signal for a Lions revival if one could call it that, for despite pressure, they were never able to breach a watertight All Blacks defence. Their meagre compensation for some good play was a penalty goal by Evans in injury time.

New Zealand therefore comfortably — more than comfortably — won their 201st international against International Board Countries and Lions, a record which underlines the strength of rugby in their part of the Souther hemisphere. Yes, the Lions were handed out a costly lesson in the basics. A frightening lesson in fact.

FIFTEENTH MATCH: HAWKES BAY
McLean Park, Napier, 6 July.
Attendance: 20,000. Weather: sunny. Pitch: hard.

Lions 25 (C. Deans, I. Paxton, D. Irwin 1 try each, 2 conversions, 1 penalty goal, J. Rutherford 1 drop goal, C. Woodward 1 penalty goal).
Hawkes Bay 19 (R. Allen, N. Porter 1 try each, L. Holmes 1 try, 2 conversions, P. O'Shaughnessy 1 drop goal).

Lions: D. Hare, T. Ringland, D. Irwin, C. Woodward, R. Ackerman, J. Rutherford, S. Smith (capt.), G. McLoughlin, C. Deans, I. Milne, S. Boyle, D. Lenihan, N. Jeavons, J. Beattie, P. Winterbottom. Reserves: I. Paxton for Beattie, H. MacNeill for Hare.

Hawkes Bay: L. Holmes, J. Frost, R. Allen, P. Dailey, P. Davis, P. O'Shaughnessy, P. Blake, N. Porter, G. Gregory, J. O'Connor, P. Fulford, G. Higginson, F. Shelford, R. Falcon, P. Anson.
Referee: T. Doocey (Canterbury).

Lions Record against Hawkes Bay
1930: Lions 14, Hawkes Bay 3.
1950: Lions 20, Hawkes Bay 0.
1959: Lions 52, Hawkes Bay 12.
1966: Lions 11, Hawkes Bay 11.
1971: Lions 25, Hawkes Bay 6.
1977: Lions 13, Hawkes Bay 11.
1983: Lions 25, Hawkes Bay 19.

SIXTEENTH MATCH: COUNTIES
Pukekohe Stadium, 9 July.
Attendance: 27,000. Weather: windy, showers. Pitch: firm.

Lions 25 (J. Carleton 1 try, O. Campbell 5 penalties, 2 drop goals).
Counties: 16 (A. Dalton 2 tries, J. Harvey 2 penalties, 1 conversion).

Lions: G. Evans, J. Carleton, J. Rutherford, M. Kiernan, R. Baird, O. Campbell, S. Smith, S. Jones, C. Fitzgerald (capt.), G. Price, D. Lenihan, S. Bainbridge, J. O'Driscoll, N. Jeavons, P. Winterbottom. Reserve: R. Ackerman for Rutherford.

Counties: T. Walsh, B. Kururangi, S. Lineen, L. Cameron, B. Robertson, J. Harvey, M. Moore, R. Ketels, A. Dalton (capt.), H. Maxwell, G. Wright, P. Tuoro, A. Dawson, T. Clarke, B. Wilson.
Referee: K. Lawrence (Bay of Plenty).

Lions Record against Counties and Combined Sides
1959: Lions 25, Counties/King Country 5.
1966: Lions 13, Counties/Thames Valley 9.
1971: Lions 25, Counties/Thames Valley 3.
1977: Lions 35, Counties/Thames Valley 10.
1983: Lions 25, Counties 16.

SEVENTEENTH MATCH: WAIKATO
Rugby Park, Hamilton, 12 July.
Attendance: 31,000. Weather: sunny, hot. Pitch: hard.

Lions 40 (O. Campbell 1 try, 4 penalty goals, 4 conversions,
C. Deans, D. Irwin, R. Laidlaw, I. Milne 1 try each).
Waikato 13 (A. Stone, B. Smith 1 try each, T. Purcell 1
penalty, R. Adam 1 conversion).

Lions: H. MacNeill, T. Ringland, D. Irwin, C. Woodward,
R. Baird, O. Campbell, R. Laidlaw, G. McLoughlin, C. Deans,
I. Milne, M. Colclough, S. Bainbridge, J. O'Driscoll (capt.),
E. Butler, P. Winterbottom. Reserves: R. Ackerman for
Woodward, G. Evans for Campbell.

Waikato: T. Purcell, R. Adam, A. Stone, C. Ellis, B. Smith,
J. Boe, G. Holmes, P. Koteka, P. Bennett, K. Searancke,
P. Wills, J. Fleming, M. Melsom, G. Tietjens, W. Bullot.
Reserves: B. Parker for Purcell, E. Brode for Bullot.
Referee: N. Whittaker (Bay of Plenty).

Lions Record against Waikato
1930: Lions 40, Waikato/Thames Valley/King Country 16.
1950: Lions 30, Waikato/Thames Valley/King Country 0.
1959: Lions 14, Waikato 0.
1966: Lions 20, Waikato 9.
1971: Lions 35, Waikato 14.
1977: Lions 18, Waikato 13.
1983: Lions 40, Waikato 13.

EIGHTEENTH MATCH: THE FOURTH TEST
Eden Park, Auckland, 16 July.
Attendance: 54,000. Weather: sunny. Pitch: fair.

Lions 6 (O. Campbell, G. Evans one penalty each).
All Blacks 38 (S. Wilson 3 tries, A. Hewson 1 try, 4 conversions, 2 penalties, A. Hayden, J. Hobbs 1 try each).

Lions: G. Evans, J. Carleton, D. Irwin, M. Kiernan, R. Baird, O. Campbell, R. Laidlaw, S. Jones, C. Fitzgerald (capt.), G. Price, M. Colclough, S. Bainbridge, J. O'Driscoll, I. Paxton, P. Winterbottom. Reserves: H. MacNeill for Campbell, R. Ackerman for Baird.

All Blacks: A. Hewson, S. Wilson, S. Pokere, W. Taylor, B. Fraser, I. Dunn, D. Loveridge, J. Ashworth, A. Dalton (capt.), G. Knight, A. Hayden, G. Whetton, M. Shaw, M. Mexted, J. Hobbs.
Referee: D. Byers (Australia).

CHAPTER 15

GOODBYE TO 1983

The hullabaloo has died down. The tour is over. Willie Johh McBride is back at his desk in a Belfast Bank, Jim Telfer returned to his teaching duties in Scotland and Ciaran Fitzgerald is again in safe harbour, behind the "exploding shells" rather than in the firing line.

The 1983 Lions are no more, just another statistic in the history of British and Irish rugby touring sides to the Southern hemisphere. The historical accounts will show them to have been one of the least successful tours, worse marginally in percentage terms to Mike Campbell-Lamberton's 1966 side in New Zealand.

I cannot speak for 1966, nor for Campbell-Lamberton who co-incidentally was also an army officer at the time. He came in for his share of criticism; the party as a whole came in for flak, but I doubt if it could have been as concentrated, as stinging, as vicious as some of the things that were written about this 1983 side and more particularly Fitzgerald.

In the cold light of day I find it incredible that one person from such a group should be singled out in such a manner — captain or not. A man who had helped inspire Ireland to Triple Crown and championship success in 1982, who also led them to a share in the championship last season and who deemed it "an honour of the highest type", found in a short ten weeks that the world of rugby can be an intensely unhappy arena too, and that when things go wrong the daggers are drawn and the "execution" carried out without trial. There was no jury. Fitzgerald was "lynched".

Fitzgerald was the choice of captain not wanted by some British journalists before the tour ever began. Fair enough. But he was selected and he should have been given the chance to develop as a player and a captain. One particularly biased scribe saw fit to castigate Fitzgerald in a most savage manner, even before arriving in New Zealand with almost one third of the tour completed! To my mind, this creep is a blot on the profession.

The captain, like everyone else in any team has to put up with criticism and I did not conceal my disappointment at times when the quality of Fitzgerald's play did not come up to scratch. One could not, for instance, make excuses for the poor quality of his line-out throwing in the first test in Christchurch or in one or two provincial games. But apart from those lapses, have no doubt about it, Fitzgerald had a good tour.

His opponents picked on the flaws exhibited by Fitzgerald in the first test and proceeded to develop a mania about it. From that day on, in the eyes of some, he could do nothing right.

While recognising that the winning of line-out possession depends to some extent on the timing of the man throwing in the ball, it must also be concluded that it has something to do with the jumpers themselves. Otherwise, for God's sake, why have big men there at all?

Robert Norster was the best of the four men there, even if each of the others, in his own particular way, was a valuable member of the group. Steve Bainbridge did develop into something like a classy Lion towards the end of the tour and Steve Boyle was a tremendous addition, for as well as being an honest player, he was the inspirational wit of the party.

The facts are however that Norster struggled with an injury and eventually had to be replaced and Bainbridge did not rise to prominence until a late stage. Boyle was certainly not the answer in the line-out and Maurice

Colclough lived for much of the ten weeks on his reputation, clearly not performing up to his capabilities.

In the remaining three tests, the Lions' problems were not Fitzgerald's crooked throws. No, the problems lay elsewhere. Norster and Colclough took a fair share of possession in that first test. They tested Andy Hayden and Gary Whetton well. They were much less efficient in the second test when Norster's back injury reared up. When Bainbridge joined Colclough for the third test he achieved some success, but not nearly enough to hamper the All Blacks. The fourth test? Forget it!

In his overall record as a player, Fitzgerald can look back with reasonable satisfaction on the tour. His play was fairly consistent, he was industrious, he absorbed physical and mental punishment and rode out the storm fairly well, although it was clear at times that he was depressed.

The depression seemed at its peak after the second test, yet he managed a moment of levity when he told his brother by telephone to "send out another flak jacket, the one I have is riddled with bullets."

After the third test he finally exploded, this time after reports of a split in the party which suggested that the various nationalities were going their own way. The personal criticism was one thing, an attack on the unit was something else entirely.

All he would say about his own critics was: "It seems to me that the accusing material is ready, pre-arranged for despatch and issued whether I play well or badly. Certain critics have gone so far over the threshold that most of their writing is in the realms of fantasy."

When it came to defending his party, his comments were much stronger. But the team had their revenge. At a party organised by the touring press in honour of the players 10 days later, the Irish, English, Scots and Welsh contingents arrived separately, suitably attired and complete with their various National emblems. They took up positions at the four corners of the room and had intended "staging" a fight when the journalist responsible for the article arrived.

Their joke backfired however as the journalist soon "smelt a rat" and left early, message received.

The team spirit is put into perspective by Michael Kiernan who tells the following story:

> We had spent two hours training in a torrential downpour before the third test. Everyone was feeling miserable as we sat on the bus awaiting our departure back to the hotel. Then one of the lads started singing, we all joined in and sang all the way back. We felt then that nobody gave a damn about us after losing the first two tests. But we had ourselves and I believe nothing, including bad results, will take away from the friendships made on that tour.

Thankfully, there were those who agreed with the assessment of Fitzgerald's worth, or at least agreed that he did not deserve to be taunted with some of the verbal utterings, which were, frankly, garbage.

John Mason of the *Daily Telegraph* was more forthright than most in his condemnation of the attacks. Writing after the third test he described Fitzgerald as "a much maligned captain who did not spare himself last Saturday. Fitzgerald is content to regard games playing, even at this august level, as a leisure pursuit. He suffers the slings and arrows of outrageous fortune with a fortitude and a shrug of the shoulders that should put the accusers to shame, not that humility would be a strong point in that quarter in any event."

Writing after the second test when Fitzgerald should have been allowed a try that might very well have changed the course of the game, Mason said:

> Had Jeff Squire and Ian Stephens been fit for the Wellington test I believe their presence would have been beneficial to the Lions. I don't suggest their absence was the difference between victory and defeat. Nor, in equal measure can I subscribe to the

well publicised theory that the bulk of the problems can be laid at the ever open door of Ciaran Fitzgerald the captain. Under persistent provocation he has maintained a dignified calm. although he must have been seething at some of the wounding barbs delivered with all the charity of a posse of piranha fish. Cast the scales from your eyes, gentlemen. This is a game, not an inquisition!

Nor was the blame for a sad tour levelled at Fitzgerald by the majority of the New Zealand press. In a tour summation, Ian Gault from the *Dominion* had this to say:

> Opposite Dalton was the captain who was not allowed to captain. Not wanted by sections of the overseas media, he was barraged, attacked and grossly underrated as a player. That he was an Irishman was bad enough, but Fitzgerald was also an army officer. Like Dalton, whom he stared in the eyes of many a scrum in five games against each other, he was a charmer. Sadly for him and the 1983 Lions, his full charms were not allowed to surface.

Further evidence came from Alex Veysey of the *New Zealand Times*:

> There was early bickering about the quality of Ciaran Fitzgerald, and this tends to be one of the divisions which occur almost traditionally in Lions touring parties. Not that it was obvious from the players, but some of the touring press certainly made a feast of the Fitzgerald/Colin Deans situation. That I felt, was a matter of insignificance compared with the lack of planning and strategy, and the defensiveness with which the Lions approached the two vital tests, the first and second.

It has been observed that Fitzgerald was not allowed to

captain. Maybe he wasn't for it was clear that the dominant force in terms of the team was coach Jim Telfer. That could have been the Irishman's biggest problem. Under pressure from the media from the start, nothing he did was good enough. He must have found it difficult to instil team spirit into his players when his own spirits were low. That he may not have been afforded the opportunity to influence the team in his own way because of Telfer's independent ways could have compounded the problem.

As a person I found Telfer to be most amiable, a straight talker and witty when he wanted to be. Yet some of the players did not get on with him. I can't relate stories of blazing rows. Neither can I say there was malicious gossip. There wasn't. What did come through loud and clear though was that the senior players were annoyed they had not more input into planning the major games while some of the younger ones felt they were being treated like schoolboys. "The annoying thing about Jim", said one prominent player, "was that he wanted to do everything by himself. It was his show. He sometimes sought us out but then proceeded to ignore any advice we had given him." Another said "The younger players, some of them at least, were actually afraid of him."

Tactically Telfer made some errors too. His orders were to play the game the New Zealand way with the centres reverting from their normal left and right positions to roles of inside and outside centres. Yet there was no consistency. for if once he acceded to requests from players, the formula was changed a few times. Then there was the fixation with using his back row to set up attacks, all very well when the squad was at full strength and when the opposition was not of the same standard. Too often they met quality opposition capable of negating the ploy even to a degree. Too often the players themselves took too much out of moves and lost chances of scoring. The backline were often criticised for their lack of flair and fluency. Sometimes they must have seethed as their forwards overplayed tactics set out for them by Telfer.

One of the players suggested another tactical error was not playing "Wednesday" and "Saturday" teams, or as near as possible to it.

Clive Woodward would be the first to agree that his form on tour was a major disappointment but he was a little upset that he went four games, or almost three weeks, without a game at one stage of the tour: "I believe the itinerary did not help the management in setting out two distinct teams, but I think they would have been better off in doing so. I appreciate that some very tough teams were met in mid-week, but that should be all the more reason why test players should be rested. I believe it wrong to play these people, too many of them at any rate, so close to a test."

Woodward put forward the theory that the "dirt-trekkers", had they been allowed to develop as a team, would have posed as much of a threat to the likes of Auckland and Canterbury as the teams which did play.

> OK, we were only beaten by a point against Auckland and although we lost, we really won the Canterbury game. However, I think the dirt-trekkers might well have done better. We are all international players and in splitting up touring teams it allows each side to develop their own distinct team spirit. It would not be a case of the likes of Canterbury going out to beat the Lions, it would be the dirt-trekkers attempting to beat Canterbury and I have no doubt WE would have won.

While Fitzgerald and Telfer were both being watched carefully for the way the playing activities were handled, manager Willie John McBride was the subject of discussion too for his straight talking at after-match press conferences. He made no bones about it. He expressed bitter disappointment with certain aspects of the New Zealand game, and with refereeing, particularly in relation to scrummaging, offside and obstruction.

He had a point. The Lions were not allowed to scrummage. The New Zealand teams they met refused to pack down quickly as British and Irish players are used to. The referees did not help the situation, often standing between the rival packs holding them apart, until, on a home put in the scrum-half decided it was time. Often the Lions, in their anxiety to pack down, charged into their opponents and often they were penalised. It was a source of frustration and annoyance to the players and to McBride.

New Zealand centres (second five eighths and centre) habitually spent their time in offside positions and chased kicks and bowled men over whether they had the ball or not. Much of it went unnoticed, or at least unpunished.

McBride, a loyal protector of his players, was quick to refer to robust and dirty play too — and there were a few nasties in New Zealand who prefer playing with heads, shoulders, backs and limbs than with the leather object which has become known as a football. Many of McBride's outbursts were quite correct and justified. Others however were badly timed and ill-advised.

McBride was a much loved figure in New Zealand and should have had the *entire* press party and *entire* New Zealand public "eating out of his hands". Like the overseas party, there were some in the New Zealand press who did not give these Lions a fair crack of the whip at any stage. They took the opportunity to seize on any weakness, on any flaw and make a meal of it. Like the time, getting wind of some of his complaints, one newspaper dubbed McBride "Whinging Willie". That must have hurt, especially since much of what he said was true.

The manager however won few friends for a subsequent attack on the New Zealand media and while McBride said he had not meant his words to apply to everyone, some of the fair-minded gentlemen of the press felt a little soured towards him.

He won no friends either by failing to comment — until it was too late — on a head-butting incident in which a North Auckland player was injured. That was the game in which Jeff Squire's interest in the tour ended and one which also signalled the finish of playing activities on tour for reserve scrum-half Nigel Melville.

A dangerous tackle on Melville looked suspiciously deliberate and McBride had no hesitation in telling the press afterwards that it was a punch. But when confronted seconds later with information on the head-butting incident which certainly looked a calculated act, he said he did not see it.

The information came from television commentator Keith Quinn, who had been in a perfect position to see and comment on it. If McBride said he did not see it, then he did not but having already singled out a North Auckland player, he should surely have made some gesture of condemnation as indeed coach Telfer did the following day, acting on information he had received.

I dealt at length with the problems faced by Fitzgerald because of the pressure created by sections of the press, as well as with the difficulties encountered as a result of poor tactics and, on a few occasions, bad selection. What could, however, in the realms of statistics, be ignored is that this Lions' side were dealt cruel blow after cruel injury blow. That, and a crazy itinerary, damaged their chances more than anything. Almost from the beginning they were hit by injury which ultimately was to rob them of several key players and throw even the best prepared tactical plans into disarray.

John O'Driscoll, one of the stars of the 1980 team in South Africa, dislocated a rib cartilage against Auckland in the second match of the tour, was out of action for a full three weeks and then struggled to find his form, only coming back to his best towards the latter end of the tour. John Carleton was out for two weeks, missing the first test because of concussion and in that game Terry Holmes tore knee ligaments, with Ian Stephens in similar trouble just a week later. Robert Norster's back injury flared up during the second test and he never played again. Jeff Squire and Nigel Melville were finished a few days later in the North

Auckland match and by then too, Stephens had been ruled out.

The end result was that after two thirds of the tour, five men had been called for as replacements or additional players. Nick Jeavons arrived as cover for John O'Driscoll and Melville as a replacement for Holmes. Then in the space of a few days, Gerry McLoughlin, Donal Lenihan and Steve Smith were flown out, McLoughlin as a replacement for Stephens and Lenihan and Smith as additional players respectively for Norster and Melville.

Jim Calder was ruled out after the third test with a broken thumb, and another to suffer from serious injury before the end was number eight, John Beattie, for whom cover arrived in the form of Eddie Butler. Then Dusty Hare dislocated his shoulder in the Hawkes Bay match after he had gone five games without a match. The blows continued when Ollie Campbell pulled a hamstring when scoring a try against Waikato and was then ineffective in the last test. Even then the problems continued, with Campbell retiring to be replaced by Hugo MacNeill and Roger Baird being helped off to be replaced by Robert Ackerman.

Injuries of that magnitude in a party generally agreed to be devoid of stars were of paramount importance to the outcome of the test series. I am not saying they would have won it. But they should have done better were they not besieged with those problems. Eleven times on tour they had to call on substitutes and on seven of those occasions two extra men were called into action. For one reason or another, and injuries generally posed a problem, the Lions fielded a total of 25 players in the four tests — a very important statistic when one compares it with the 16 used by the All Blacks. The New Zealanders from the very beginning were a more settled side and once they had got over the hiccups experienced in the first test, that began to assert itself more and more as an advantage.

The itinerary was not calculated to help. Indeed All Black captain Andy Dalton said he was astounded that the four home countries tours committee accepted it in the form in which it took: "As an All Black, if I were facing something similar I would most definitely have sought to change it were it within my powers to do so. In the circumstances I think they have done well. To go into only the second game against a side as strong as Auckland and then continue to play midweek games against top opposition seemed crazy to me, but accept it they did."

The New Zealand Rugby Union certainly made a financial killing, for with mid-week games in three large centres such as Auckland, Christchurch and Wellington as well as tests in the same cities, they got the crowds out. In the smaller cities the weekend fans surfaced in droves too, so the N.Z.R.U. won on both counts and they laughed all the way to the bank. Lions, the players on £8 a day pocket money, struggled on, although because of New Zealand hospitality and their own confined social life, most of their struggling was done on the pitch.

Certainly the tours committee should be held responsible in some degree for difficulties, which with a little determined persuasion could well have been eased.

The state of New Zealand rugby is strong and the Lions for the first time ever did not play any combined sides on their provincial round-up. That made their task even more difficult again because there was more cohesion in the opposition and more pride at stake for them.

McBride and Telfer succeeded evidently in one or two changes in the itinerary. They asked for more but their requests were not entertained. The manager, at the dinner following the third test, said more thought should go into the drawing up of fixtures in future tours. The timing of his remarks may have sounded as if he was "whinging" again, but in fairness to him, he had said it before the party left and so often in the early stages of the tour as to make one believe he would still not have been happy had they won the lot.

His speech did not go unnoticed by the four home unions committee whose chairman, Micky Steele-Bolger, was in New Zealand. He reacted strongly to McBride's comments, saying that had the matches been won, the manager would not have complained; that he knew the extent of the itinerary before the trip and that he had accepted it. Maybe he did. He obviously did, but I genuinely believe that both McBride and Telfer made a bigger play than may be generally known to have major alterations made, but failed. As a management team, they would not have the influence to have those changes made against the will of whoever wanted it set that way for one reason or another.

Undoubtedly these 1983 Lions — one of the most conscientious and popular touring sides of all time — contributed to their own downfall. There were times when the forwards played well, and the backs badly, and vice versa. The instances of everyone hitting a peak together were rare enough, too rare in fact, but behind that comment is a feeling of pity for these lost Lions who tried so hard but, taking the injuries in particular into account, were just not good enough for a series win.

That series is where success or failure is judged and the results speak for themselves. But according to Andy Dalton, who agrees the tour was a failure, "it is a harsh reflection on the side, for looking back at the tests we can count ourselves fortunate to have won the first, which, as far as I am concerned, decided the series."

But New Zealand rugby is alive and well, while the game in Britain and Ireland must improve dramatically to keep pace. Otherwise Jim Telfer's advice to his successor as Lions coach will be to "take out a big insurance policy".

CHAPTER 16

PROFILES OF THE LIONS

FULL BACKS

Hugo MacNeill (Ireland). Established himself as the number one full back and was first choice for the opening tests. Hugo however did not play exceptionally well overall, although his defence was generally solid. His main problem concerned the timing of his incursions into the line and he accepted his exclusion from the team to meet the All Blacks in the third test in a philosophical manner. The team was announced only a day after MacNeill's confidence was wrecked following a disastrous goal kicking display against Canterbury. He returned, however, as a substitute in the fourth test and while his attempted flip on pass to Robert Ackerman was seized upon by Stu Wilson, he will be remembered for one bone-crunching tackle on Steve Pokere which won him generous applause from the crowd. Off the field, Hugo was the official minder of "Larry" the Lions' mascot, and a member of the social committee which automatically gave him the right to serve on the "jury" during "court" sessions.

Dusty Hare (England). Finished as second highest scorer of the tour to Ollie Campbell with 88 points, an average of 14.6. Kicked many vital points for the Lions in the six matches he played in, but must have been disappointed at not getting more games. Played five times in the first nine games, but did not get another run until after the third test and in that game his tour ended when he collided with a Hawkes Bay player and dislocated his shoulder. Another member of the "jury" and thus immune from "prosecution".

UTILITY BACK

Gwyn Evans (Wales). For a man who went out on tour without a specific role, Evans was one of the successes of the backline. He played on the left and right wings and out-half before winning his test place at full back instead of MacNeill. Even then his roving was not finished because he moved back to out-half when Ollie Campbell limped off in the fourth test. Off the pitch he was friendly and quiet. 12 appearances.

WINGERS

John Carleton (England). Top try scorer with nine, and unlucky indeed not to have got a few more. Missed the first test through injury but came back to make a good impact on the tour and had the backline reached their potential together more, he would obviously have benefited. Played 11 matches and hundreds of pool games — with much less success!

Trevor Ringland (Ireland). Ringland had an exceptionally good tour. He deputised well for Carleton in the first test and although written off by the usual "moaners" after one poor display early in the tour, got on top of his game quickly afterwards. He went from strength to strength and long before the finish had truly answered his few critics. With two tries in the Manawatu game, he finally got five in nine appearances and contributed to a number of others. He was the "prosecutor" on "court" day. An avid sportsman, he tried his hand at wild pig hunting. He shot one: a rock!

Roger Baird (Scotland). Looked the fastest player on the team and if he did not have the physical presence to match his speed, he made the most of his attributes. Baird did little wrong, and when the chances came his way he took them. His pace told in the Wellington match when he scored twice and also in the third test when he scored the Lions' first try, leaving several defenders in his wake. Baird was first choice left-winger in 11 games.

CENTRES

Robert Ackerman (Wales). One felt sorry for the centres on this tour because the selectorial policy was such that they must not have known where they stood. Whether this affected Ackerman's performances is a matter for debate, but in my opinion he was a little disappointing. Defensively strong and always willing, he lacked that little bit of sparkle. Played 10 games, including two tests (one as a substitute). He was first choice centre on five occasions, played twice as a sub there and made three appearances on the left-wing, once as a stand-in. Scored his only try from that position.

Michael Kiernan (Ireland). A controversial exclusion from the first test side, Kiernan looked the biggest dangerman in the early stages of the tour. He made two tries and scored the winner against Wellington but the management dropped a "bombshell" by leaving him out of the first test. He came back, however, for the remaining three games and overall had a good tour, even if the early promise he showed did not always materialise. A better player than a singer evidently, as the "court" was to hear. Ten appearances, all as first choice centre.

Clive Woodward (England). One of the forgotten men of the tour, playing only seven games. He was not at his best although in the last provincial game against Waikato, he hit a peak. I'm sure he knows more than anyone that it should have happened sooner and he did get a chance to prove himself with two big games in succession early on — against Auckland and Bay of Plenty. "Woody" did accept his fate however and enjoyed the tour to the full.

David Irwin (Ireland). With six tries he was the highest scorer of the four centres and joint second of the party with Roger Baird. The strong running Irwin took great joy in grabbing those tries and in the celebrations following those than anyone else. Looked set at one stage to have a spectacular tour but ended up enjoying only a reasonably satisfactory one. He was consistent, however, and while few will look back with any satisfaction on the last game, when he came in to make his third test appearance for the injured John Rutherford, Irwin can to some extent, particularly for his exceptionally good defence. Eleven games in all. Not bad at pool and an expert wangler in "court"!

OUT-HALVES

Ollie Campbell (Ireland). If there was a criticism of Ollie Campbell, it can only be that he did not wear the fashionable thermal vest or wrap plastic around his feet in the third test in Dunedin. He confessed afterwards to have been "freezing cold" during the match and that perhaps explained why his tactical kicking was not up to his usual high standards. Campbell, of course, was rather confined in the four tests — confined to four penalty goals and one drop goal. But he did produce some magical attacking moments and defensively his game was as strong as ever it was. The highlight for me was certainly the only try he scored — against Waikato — when he danced his way through several bemused defenders. Eleven appearances and the top scorer with 124 points. One appearance in "court" where his punishment for being too pale was to wear a dark pair of tights for an evening.

John Rutherford (Scotland). Like Campbell, Rutherford

227

proved his worth on the tour and eventually he was found too valuable to let out of the side, being drafted in for the third test, during which he scored one of the two Lions tries. Had a couple of forgettable games, but generally his play was of excellent quality. He made a total of 10 appearances, three of them in the middle of the field. Another member of the jury.

SCRUM-HALVES

Terry Holmes (Wales). Must have been destined not to complete a Lions tour. After injury forced him home from South Africa in 1980, the jinx struck again for this player who has been classed as the best scrum-half in the world. The world title "fight" between himself and Dave Loveridge never materialised because Holmes damaged knee ligaments early in the first test and that was it. His loss was incalculable. In all, he played only about 200 minutes of rugby spread over four games. One try.

Roy Laidlaw (Scotland). Many felt Laidlaw had a poor tour and in some ways he did. His passing was often inconsistent and he made mistakes under pressure. But many may forget that Laidlaw had an extremely tough trip and unlike the vast majority of the players, rarely got time to relax. Because of the injury to Holmes and subsequently to his replacement, Nigel Melville, Laidlaw hardly had any rest, playing five matches in succession including and between the second and third tests. It was only then that he earned his first week off. In between his off days, he had a few memorable matches and indeed at one stage looked like pushing Holmes for his test place. He made a total of 13 appearances.

Nigel Melville (England). We will never know just what influence this young Englishman may have had on the Lions. Made a superb début in the rout of Southland at Invircargill and looked to be shaping up as a brilliant player, which my English colleagues will say he is anyway. The scrum-half problems did not end with Holmes returning home, for in his second match, Melville was injured and the neck damage was severe enough to sideline him for the remaining three weeks. "Smelly" to his friends. Nothing sinister in it, just that it rhymes with "Melly". Two appearances, two tries.

Steve Smith (England). The man who nearly became a Lion in 1980, got a false alarm in 1983, and finally made it. His tour appearances were confined to two, but he was honoured with the captaincy for one of them and inspired the Lions to a win over Hawkes Bay. Definitely one of the more flamboyant members of the party.

PROPS

Graham Price (Wales). The man who fought his way back into the Welsh team was rewarded with his place on the Lions party and was an ever present in the test side, making six more appearances in provincial matches. Early on there was no contest between himself and Iain Milne for the tight head berth, but I got the feeling that Price faded somewhat as the tour progressed and was not the dominant figure he had been in past tours.

Iain Milne (Scotland). "The Bear" as he was known, improved considerably as the tour wore on. He sometimes looked unfit in the early games but mobility returned and he was rewarded for some fine off-the-ball running with his only try against Waikato. Always popular with his colleagues, I wonder why? Of course, he was after all, the "judge"!

Ian Stephens (Wales). Proved a point to the Welsh selectors by winning a place in the test side after being dropped for Staff Jones. He worked hard after the international championship to get superbly fit and made an impact in the first test. Even when injured in the Southland game he dedicated himself to hours of intense training in a bid to recover. Sadly, however, his tour ended when he aggravated his knee ligament injury in training at Wangarei 11 days later.

Staff Jones (Wales). While Stephens deservedly won the race for a test place, Jones surely is worthy of mention for resilience at least. Like Laidlaw, he had to endure an exhausting period midway through the tour when he played in seven consecutive matches. He played in the last three tests and while he coped adequately, was not as effective as Stephens had been in the first.

Gerry McLoughlin (Ireland). Took particular delight in being called up as a replacement, even if it was for a short period and even if he played just two games. Took a while to get going in the first, but had a great second half and did well too in his next game — very well, considering he was playing out of his normal position of tight head prop. "Ginger" quickly established himself as one of the characters of the party and there were many willing helpers to rescue him and his dislocated toe from the "depths" of a Jacuzzi pool on the Sunday morning after the final test.

HOOKERS

Ciaran Fitzgerald (Ireland). CAPTAIN. Was not always in a position to be the cheerful figure he became known as throughout Ireland's successful spell. He had his problems, brought on by savage criticism more than anything else. Yet he showed himself to be a man of character for although obviously deeply hurt, he got on with his job as best he could. There must have been times when the criticism was unbearable, but if it was reflected a couple of times in his play, there were also times when Fitzgerald's individual performances spurred the Lions on to memorable wins. He was desperately unlucky not to have been awarded a try in the second test in Wellington just before half-time, when the score stood at 9-0 for the All Blacks. The try was legitimate but referee Francis Palmade blew too early for an infringement by All Black Allan Hewson. That might well have been the turning point of the game. It also escaped the critics that he out-hooked All Black captain Andy Dalton 2-1 in the five games (one v. Counties) they met in and that the total tighthead duel in favour of Fitzgerald in all his 11 matches was 12-2. In his role as captain, Fitzgerald had many off the field duties, most of them speechmaking. In every aspect he proved himself a fine ambassador for the Lions.

Colin Deans (Scotland). Deans appeared in the remaining seven matches and in some ways put pressure on Fitzgerald immediately by taking five tightheads against Bay of Plenty when in opposition to the man many fancied as the New Zealand test hooker, Hika Reid. He was not always as spectacular however and though an invaluable member of any side he played in, I think it would have been a retrograde step for the management to have considered ousting Fitzgerald or indeed for the captain himself to have stepped down. The Scotsman had his own difficulties, having learned of the birth of his second child only a week after arriving and then having to sit out the test games in the stands. He accepted his lot however without complaining. He scored two tries.

SECOND ROWS

Maurice Colclough (England). Expected to be one of the stars of the side, Colclough was, frankly, a disappointment. He worked hard to regain full fitness after a knee operation in January had threatened to end his career, and he did have a few exceptionally good games. He was unable to establish himself with any real consistency however, and was generally outplayed out of touch in all but the first of his four test appearances. Indeed he may have come under some pressure to retain his place for the fourth test were it not for reserving his best form for the Waikato game. A total of 11 appearances.

Robert Norster (Wales). Looked the best of the four second rows until injury cut short his participation and thus his contribution was confined to six matches, including two tests. A quick talker with a sense of humour, he induced a waitress to write down automatically "and a bucket of water for the horse" in one particular hotel dining room.

Steve Boyle (England). Never really looked like making the test side, but he was one helluva tourist. Strange that an Englishman — no slight intended — should be the life and soul of the party, but if Boyle had a few competitors, he certainly dominated the entertainment section of the tour. Nicknamed "Foggy" because of his ability to shout while talking, he was as committed to the success of the tour as anyone, even though at times he must have felt he was the forgotten one. He played in the first two matches, went five more without a game and finally ended up playing in six. He opened up his own "travel agency" — *Fog's Tours* — as he and the players believed he was running his own trip. On the last day, Boyle was the recipient of a presentation for being the most humorous member of the party. He proved it by presenting the management team with three pairs of dark sun-glasses and three white canes — just to let them know how he felt about his exclusion from the remaining 12 games!

Steve Bainbridge (England). Came into the party as a reserve for Donal Lenihan and although he won some great line-out possession in the odd provincial game, did not look test material — that is until he was called in for the third game, when Norster was injured. He had a fine test. That was his graduation and if the latter stage of the tour is a good indication, then he was probably the most improved forward in the party. In all, he played 11 games, and thousands more off the pitch (video). But he did not like losing to machines and became known as "the moaner"!

Donal Lenihan (Ireland). It will never be known just what sort of influence Lenihan could have had on the party had he been there from the beginning. He was bitterly disappointed at having to withdraw before the start of the tour, but he had some measure of compensation when called upon as an additional player on foot of Norster's injury. It was too late for him to mount a realistic challenge for a test place, but he gave it his best shot and must, at one stage of the week leading up to the last test, have had Colclough somewhat worried, when it became apparent that he and not Bainbridge would have to fight for retention of his position. Serious challenger to Boyle as a comedian.

FLANKERS

Jeff Squire (Wales). Undoubtedly the one whom the Lions needed most. An immaculate footballer, a tower of strength, Squire's departure with a damaged shoulder came as a crushing blow to the tourists. In six appearances he scored two tries, but his overall contribution was greater. Undoubtedly he could have been one of the greats of this side. In the short few games he had, he was a major success and he was a sad, sad loss.

John O'Driscoll (Ireland). The early injury was another setback for the Lions and for the player himself, but he had begun to put his game together again in the latter stages of the tour. His "friend" once again travelled with him and on more than one occasion he had to face the jury to explain the activities of his sometimes unruly companion. Captained the side twice in his eight matches, two of them tests.

Peter Winterbottom (England). A consistently good player, Winterbottom earned himself the respect of the New Zealand public with some tremendous displays, particularly

233

in the final test when he was one of the few Lions to shine. An ever present in the test line-up, "strawman" was undoubtedly one of the stars.

Jim Calder (Scotland). Having won his way into the test team for the third of the series, Calder suffered an unfortunate injury to his thumb which proved the end of the road for him. Brought in as blind side flanker for the third test, he had hopes of retaining his place, but it was not to be. He played seven games and had the respectable total of three tries for his efforts.

Nick Jeavons (England). Jeavons was the first of the replacements to arrive in New Zealand and he, and Dusty Hare were the only ones to have played in six or more matches without being on a losing side. Jeavons' form was not always consistent even if he showed some nice touches of football at times.

NUMBER EIGHTS

Iain Paxton (Scotland). Was worried at the start of the tour that he might not make the test team. He was, however, a cut above his rival, John Beattie, and there was little doubt that he deserved his place. Injured in the second game, he was replaced by Beattie but fought back to fitness and regained his place for the last two, although some believe he may not have been fully fit in the fourth game as he had suffered a further injury in the meantime.

John Beattie (Scotland). Looked promising at times, but often tended to take too much out of the ball at the back of the scrum. Like Paxton he played nine times on tour.

Eddie Butler (Wales). The Welsh captain was called out when Beattie damaged a groin in the Hawkes Bay game and his only outing was against Waikato when he distinguished himself quite well.

APPENDICES

1983 LIONS RECORD AT A GLANCE

Beat Wanganui	47-15
Lost to Auckland	12-13
Beat Bay of Plenty	34-16
Beat Wellington	27-19
Beat Manawatu	25-18
Beat Mid Canterbury	26-6
Lost to New Zealand	12-16
Beat West Coast	52-16
Beat Southland	41-3
Beat Wairarapa-Bush	57-10
Lost to New Zealand	0-9
Beat North Auckland	21-12
Lost to Canterbury	20-22
Lost to New Zealand	8-15
Beat Hawkes Bay	25-19
Beat Counties	25-16
Beat Waikato	40-13
Lost to New Zealand	6-38

Played 18. Won 12. Lost 6. For 478 Points, Against 276 Points.

INDIVIDUAL SCORING

	Tries	Conversions	Penalties	Drop Goals	Total
O. Campbell	1	18	22	6	124
D. Hare	—	17	18	—	88
J. Carleton	9	—	—	—	36
R. Baird	6	—	—	—	24
D. Irwin	6	—	—	—	24
J. Rutherford	2	—	—	5	23
G. Evans	3	3	1	—	21
T. Ringland	5	—	—	—	20
J. Beattie	4	—	—	—	16
I. Paxton	4	—	—	—	16
J. Calder	3	—	—	—	12
M. Kiernan	2	—	—	—	11
H. MacNeill	—	1	2	—	8
J. Squire	2	—	—	—	8
N. Melville	2	—	—	—	8
R. Laidlaw	2	—	—	—	8
C. Deans	2	—	—	—	8
P. Winterbottom	1	—	—	—	4
R. Ackerman	1	—	—	—	4
T. Holmes	1	—	—	—	4
I. Stephens	1	—	—	—	4
I. Milne	1	—	—	—	4
C. Woodward	—	—	1	—	3
	58	39	44	12	478 pts.

S. Jones, C. Fitzgerald, M. Colclough, S. Bainbridge, G. Price, R. Norster, J. O'Driscoll, N. Jeavons, S. Boyle, S. Smith, D. Lenihan and G. McLoughlin were the Lions who did not score.

Opponents scored a total of 30 tries, 18 conversions, 34 penalties and six drop goals.

INDIVIDUAL PLAYING RECORDS

BACKS	Wanganui	Auckland	Bay of Plenty	Wellington	Manawatu	Mid Canterbury	1st Test	West Coast
D. Hare (E)	F/B		F/B			F/B		F/B
H. MacNeill (I)		F/B		F/B	F/B		F/B	
G. Evans (W)	L/W	F/B•		R/W•		L/W		L/W
R. Baird (S)		L/W		L/W	L/W		L/W	
T. Ringland (I)	R/W		L/W		R/W	R/W	R/W	
J. Carleton (E)		R/W	R/W	R/W				R/W
M. Kiernan (I)	C			C	C			
C. Woodward (E)		C	C			C		C
R. Ackerman (W)	C		C		C		C	C
D. Irwin (I)		C		C		C	C	
O. Campbell (I)		O/H		O/H	O/H		O/H	
J. Rutherford (S)	O/H		O/H			O/H		O/H
T. Holmes (W)		S/H		S/H		S/H	S/H	
R. Laidlaw (S)	S/H		S/H	S/H•	S/H		S/H•	S/H
*N. Melville (E)								
*S. Smith (E)								

*Replacement Player   • Reserve during game

Southland	Wairarapa-Bush	2nd Test	North Auckland	Canterbury	3rd Test	Hawkes Bay	Counties	Waikato	4th Test	Total
F/B						F/B				6
		F/B		F/B		F/B.		F/B	F/B.	9
F/B.	F/B		F/B		F/B		F/B	O/H.	F/B	12
	L/W	L/W		L/W	L/W		L/W	L/W	L/W	11
L/W			R/W			R/W		R/W		9
R/W	R/W	R/W		R/W	R/W		R/W		R/W	11
C	C	C	C		C		C		C	10
				C		C		C		7
			L/W			L/W	C.	C.	L/W.	10
C	C	C		C		C		C	C	11
	O/H	O/H	O/H		O/H		O/H	O/H	O/H	11
O/H			C	O/H	C	O/H	C			10
										4
	S/H	S/H	S/H.	S/H	S/H			S/H	S/H	13
S/H			S/H							2
						S/H	S/H			2

INDIVIDUAL PLAYING RECORDS

FORWARDS	Wanganui	Auckland	Bay of Plenty	Wellington	Manawatu	Mid Canterbury	1st Test	West Coast
I. Stephens (W)			P		P		P	
S. Jones (W)	P	P		P		P		P
G. Price (W)		P		P	P	P		
I. Milne (S)	P		P			P		P
(I) *G. McLoughlin								
C. Fitzgerald (I)	H	H		H	H		H	
C. Deans (S)			H			H		H
M. Colclough (E)			S/R	S/R	S/R	S/R	S/R	
S. Bainbridge (E)		S/R	S/R			S/R		S/R
R. Norster (W)	S/R			S/R	S/R		S/R	
S. Boyle (E)	S/R	S/R						S/R
*D. Lenihan (I)								
J. Squire (W)	W/F		W/F	W/F	W/F		W/F	
J. O'Driscoll (I)		W/F						
(E) P. Winterbottom	W/F			W/F	W/F		W/F	
J. Calder (S)		W/F	W/F			W/F		W/F
*N. Jeavons (E)						W/F		W/F
J. Beattie (S)	No. 8	No. 8		No. 8		No. 8		No. 8
I. Paxton (S)			No. 8		No. 8		No. 8	
*E. Butler (W)								

Replacement Player   • *Reserve during game.*

Southland	Wairarapa-Bush	2nd Test	North Auckland	Canterbury	3rd Test	Hawkes Bay	Counties	Waikato	4th Test	Total
P										4
P.	P	P	P	P	P		P		P	13
P		P	P		P		P		P	10
	P			P		P		P		8
						P		P		2
H		H	H		H		H		H	11
	H			H		H		H		7
S/R		S/R		S/R	S/R			S/R	S/R	11
	S/R		S/R	S/R	S/R		S/R	S/R	S/R	11
S/R		S/R								6
	S/R		S/R			S/R				6
						S/R	S/R			2
			No. 8							6
W/F	W/F	W/F		W/F			W/F	W/F	W/F	8
	W/F	W/F		W/F	W/F	W/F	W/F	W/F	W/F	12
W/F			W/F	W/F						7
	W/F.		W/F			W/F	No. 8			6
	No. 8	No. 8	No. 8			No. 8				9
No. 8		No. 8		No. 8	No. 8	No. 8			No. 8	9
								No. 8		1

243

THE IRISH RUGBY TOURISTS

R. Alexander (NIFC) 1938
W. J. Ashby (UCC) 1910

G. Beamish (Leicester, RAF) 1930
C. A. Boyd (Trinity) 1896
C. V. Boyle (Trinity) 1938
M. J. Bradley (Dolphin) 1924
T. N. Brand (NIFC) 1924
B. Bresnihan (UCD) 1966/68
N. Brophy (Blackrock) 1959/62
L. Bulger (Lansdowne) 1896

O. Campbell (Old Belvedere) 1980/83
T. Clifford (Young Munster) 1950
A. D. Clinch (Wanderers) 1896
J. Clinch (Wanderers) 1924
T. Crean (Wanderers) 1896
G. E. Cromey (Queen's) 1938
W. Cunningham (Lansdowne) 1924

I. G. Davidson (NIFC) 1903
R. Dawson (Wanderers) 1959
G. P. Doran (Lansdowne) 1899
M. Doyle (Blackrock) 1968
W. Duggan (Blackrock) 1977
M. J. Dunne (Lansdowne) 1930

M. English (Bohemians) 1959
R. W. Edwards (Malone) 1904

J. L. Farrell (Bective) 1930
C. Fitzgerald (St Mary's) 1983
A. R. Foster (Derry) 1910

M. Gibson (Cambridge Univ/NIFC) 1966/68/71/74/77
K. Goodall (Derry) 1968
T. Grace (St Mary's) 1974
C. R. Graves (Wanderers) 1938

N. Henderson (Queen's) 1950
D. Hewitt (Queen's) 1959/62
M. Hipwell (Terenure) 1971
W. Hunter (CIYMS) 1962

D. Irwin (Instonians) 1983

R. Johnston (Wanderers) 1896

M. Keane (Lansdowne) 1977
K. Kennedy (CIYMS/London Irish) 1966/74
M. Kiernan (Dolphin) 1983
T. J. Kiernan (UCC and Constitution) 1962/68
J. Kyle (Queen's) 1950

R. Lamont (Instonians) 1966
M. Lane (UCC) 1950
D. Lenihan (Constitution) 1983
S. Lynch (St Mary's) 1971

W. J. McBride (Ballymena) 1962/66/68/71/74
J. McCarthy (Dolphin) 1950
A. N. McClinton (NIFC) 1910
T. M. McGown (NIFC) 1899
B. McKay (Queen's) 1950
H. McKibbin (Queen's) 1938
S. McKinney (Dungannon) 1974
G. McLoughlin (Shannon) 1983
R. McLoughlin (Gosforth/Blackrock) 1966/71
H. MacNeill (Oxford Univ/Blackrock) 1983
J. V. McVicker (Collegians) 1924
J. Magee (Bective) 1896
L. Magee (Bective) 1896

E. Martelli (Trinity) 1899
B. S. Massey (Hull, and Ulster) 1904
R. B. Mayne (Queen's) 1938
A. D. Meares (Trinity) 1896
S. Millar (Ballymena) 1959/1962/1968
D. Milliken (Bangor) 1974
J. Moloney (St Mary's) 1974
G. J. Morgan (Clontarf) 1938
W. Mulcahy (UCD/Bohemians/Bective) 1959/62
K. Mullen (Old Belvedere) 1950
A. Mulligan (Wanderers/London Irish) 1959
N. A. Murphy (Constitution) 1959/66
P. F. Murray (Wanderers) 1930

J. Nelson (Malone) 1950
G. Norton (Bective) 1950

R. O'Donnell (St Mary's) 1980
J. O'Driscoll (London Irish/Manchester) 1980/83
H. O. H. O'Neill (Queen's) 1930
A. J. O'Reilly (Old Belvedere) 1955/59
P. Orr (Old Wesley) 1977/1980

C. D. Patterson (Malone) 1904
C. S. Patterson (Instonians) 1980
C. Pedlow (Queen's) 1955
O. J. S. Piper (Constitution) 1910

T. Reid (Garryowen) 1955
J. Robbie (Greystones) 1980
R. Roe (Lansdowne) 1955
W. J. Roche (UCC/Newport) 1924
T. Ringland (Ballymena) 1983

J. W. Sealy (Trinity) 1896
F. Slattery (Blackrock) 1971/74
R. S. Smyth (Trinity) 1903
T. Smyth (Newport) 1910

A. Tedford (Malone) 1903
R. H. Thompson (Instonians) 1955
C. Tucker (Shannon) 1980
W. Tyrrell (Queen's) 1910

S. Walker (Instonians) 1955
James Wallace (Wanderers) 1903
Joseph Wallace (Wanderers) 1903
J. Walsh (Sunday's Well) 1966
T. Ward (Garryowen/St Mary's) 1980
G. Wood (Garryowen) 1959

R. Young (Queen's) 1966/68